Praise for
The Quickwrite Handbook

"I used to think I knew what quickwrites were until I met Linda Rief. Linda makes mentor authors accessible and makes putting words on a page possible as she lovingly nudges us all toward a belief in our potential as writers. Everything with Linda is an invitation and you can't help but RSVP, 'Yes! I can do this!' This book will move your writing, your student writers, and your teaching to new places."

—Sara K. Ahmed, author of *Being the Change* and coauthor of *Upstanders*

"Linda Rief models the essential moves a teacher must make to increase engagement and joy in writing in The Quickwrite Handbook. And here's a confession: it took me a long time to read this book. It seems small, but it is packed with invitations I dare you to resist. Linda has an uncanny ability for finding texts that create an urgency for study and imitation. I wrote next to her sample texts, her ideas, and her stunning student examples for weeks. You simply must have this book."

—Penny Kittle, English teacher, coauthor of *180 Days*, and author of *Book Love*

"In this valuable resource, Linda Rief shares the models from literature that inspire her students and exactly how she uses them. The mentor texts in this book are jumping-off places. They build vision for what strong writing looks and feels and tastes like. They provide the necessary scaffolding that will allow young writers to outgrow themselves and create something they (and we) can be proud of."

—Ralph Fletcher, author of *Joy Write* and coauthor of *Writing Workshop*

"Perhaps you have had the experience of finding that your car will not start because the battery is dead. Maybe you said a few choice words or stomped around a bit before you paused to take a breath and think. It is likely that you phoned someone who came with jumper cables and hooked the battery of your car to the battery of their car. Then, you took another breath, opened the driver's door, and sat down behind the wheel. And when the ignition switch rewarded you with the purr of your engine you exhaled with relief. Linda Rief's book is that friend with the jumper cables coming to the rescue. Her text is filled with sage advice that is steeped in years of classroom practice and Linda's calming manner. She offers each of us a clear and concise guide to understanding why quickwrites work and how to give them power in our daily practice."

—Lester Laminack, coauthor of *Writers ARE Readers* and *Bullying Hurts*

Twitter Dec 03

I learned about quickwrites from @LindaMRief
20 years ago . . . and my classroom
has never been the same.
@pennykittle

꒰

LINDA RIEF

THE
Quickwrite
HANDBOOK

MENTOR TEXTS
to Jumpstart Your Students' Thinking and Writing

HEINEMANN
Portsmouth, NH

Heinemann

361 Hanover Street

Portsmouth, NH 03801–3912

www.heinemann.com

Offices and agents throughout the world

The author and publisher wish to thank those who have generously given permission to reprint borrowed material:

"Getting It Right" from *Jesus Was a Homeboy* by Kevin Carey. Copyright © 2016 by Kevin Carey. Reprinted with the permission of The Permissions Company, Inc., on behalf of CavanKerry Press, www.cavankerrypress.org.

credits continue on page 186

Library of Congress Cataloging-in-Publication Data

Names: Rief, Linda, author.

Title: The quickwrite handbook : 100 mentor texts to jumpstart your students' thinking and writing / Linda Rief.

Description: Portsmouth : Heinemann, [2018] | Includes bibliographical references.

Identifiers: LCCN 2018005852 | ISBN 9780325098128

Subjects: LCSH: English language—Composition and exercises—Study and teaching (Elementary) | English language—Composition and exercises—Study and teaching (Middle school)

Classification: LCC LB1576 .R5196 2018 | DDC 372.6—dc23

LC record available at https://lccn.loc.gov/2018005852

Editor: Sue Paro

Production: Hilary Goff

Cover design: Suzanne Heiser

Interior design: Monica Ann Crigler

Typesetter: Gina Poirier Design

Photography: Sherry Day and Michael Grover

Manufacturing: Steve Bernier

Printed in the United States of America on acid-free paper

22 21 20 19   VP   4 5

Contents

Beyond Self   97

Acknowledgments

Penny Kittle, a teacher at Kennett High School in North Conway, New Hampshire, and Tom Romano, a professor at Miami University in Ohio, are good friends and colleagues who are the most generous educators I know. My email is often filled with book titles, articles, excerpts from novels, poems, op-ed essays or interviews, all sent with "Have you seen this? Thought you might like it!" They send me pieces of their students' writing and videos they have produced. I try to reciprocate with anything I find that might be of interest to them. I have lost track of who sent what to whom. Neither Tom nor Penny would ever claim ownership and say, "I sent that to you," because they are all about sharing anything that will help kids grow as readers and writers. I am forever grateful for the conversations we have, the materials we share, and their friendship that make them far more than colleagues.

Kylene Beers and Bob Probst push my thinking as a reader and writer, each time I hear them speak. What are the connections? How can I make what I do more meaningful to the kids as readers, as well as writers? Working with Kylene and Bob, Penny, and Chris Crutcher, for a good portion of each summer over the last ten years energizes me to continually reflect on and strengthen those critical issues that matter most as we work with our students. They have always made me feel that the quickwrites students produce from compelling mentor texts are truly remarkable and a noteworthy technique that gets even the most reluctant kids thinking and writing.

Emily Geltz and Chris Hall, both former interns with me and now colleagues at Oyster River Middle School, have often shared the mentor texts that work best with their fifth- and sixth-grade students. I know also that Emily and Chris are writers and readers, always sharing with their students their thinking processes as they write and read.

I am grateful to all those teachers who have either been in courses at the University of New Hampshire Summer Literacy Institute with me or in workshops throughout the year, for letting me know what mentor texts worked best with their students and for them as writers, and mentioning other pieces they have added to their collections:

Debra Drew and Caitlin Evans, teachers at Perrysburg High School in Perrysburg, Ohio

~ x ᔕ

Kristina Peterson and Dennis Magliozzi, teachers at Exeter High School in Exeter, New Hampshire

Linda Becker, former teacher and colleague at Oyster River Middle School, for letting me share her daughter Abigail's beautiful writing

Jessica Ryan, Catherine Flynn, Lynn Adams, Erin Warren, Nita Kulesa, Michael McPake, Emily Geltz, Alyssa Eckhardt, and Brittany McNary Thurman, all classroom teachers, for letting me include the poignant pieces of writing they crafted from mentor texts I shared with them in courses or workshops

Penny Kittle, Ralph Fletcher, Sara Ahmed, and Lester Laminack, for reading the manuscript and responding with such thoughtful comments in recommending this book to others. Ralph Fletcher told me he does not write recommendations for professional books, but since I had three of his four sons in my eighth grade Language Arts class, he considered me "grand-mothered in."

I am most grateful to my eighth-grade students for letting me share their thinking throughout these pages. It is their hard work and tenacity at writing honestly and thoughtfully that energizes me each day to continue in the classroom. I want their voices heard. Our young people, no matter what their ages, have important things to say and we need to find every opportunity to encourage them to communicate their ideas. It is through their thinking, their imaginations, their beliefs, and their feelings that we will solve the problems that still exist throughout the world.

To all of the Heinemann staff that worked on this book, I am so grateful for your positive comments, your suggestions, and your expertise that clarified and enriched all I wanted to say and that always kept this book moving forward:

Lisa Fowler, VP and Publisher
Sue Paro, Senior Project Manager
Hilary Goff, Senior Production Editor
Edie Davis Quinn, Editorial Coordinator
Josh Evans, Product Manager
Sherry Day, Video Producer and Photographer
Michael Grover, Video Producer and Photographer
Suzanne Heiser, Cover Designer
Monica Crigler, Interior Designer

A Note to Teachers

ॐ

I hope this book shows you what students are capable of doing as writers and artists, as readers and creative thinkers. The mentor pieces included here are the ones that jumpstart my students' thinking. They are the pieces from which my students craft the most writing, the strongest writing. Your students most certainly can do this also. I am lending you the writing that has worked for us. Use these until you find the mentor pieces that work best with your students. Then add your writing and your students' writing to this collection so that you have a repertoire of pieces that resonate strongly with your students. That's the writing from which your students will really benefit.

You will notice several different ways of framing each page. All pages have the mentor text and the Try This section. Others have added information that is meant to help you and your students see how these quickwrites were extended in various ways.

Mentor Piece and Try This For your students (and you), from which to do a quickwrite.

Interludes Examples for you and your students of how the writing developed beyond the quickwrite.

Teacher Notes Additional information about how I use these mentor pieces beyond the Try This, or some background information that might be useful or interesting to you or your students, either before or after they have done the quickwrite.

In the workshop we (Kylene Beers, Bob Probst, Penny Kittle, Chris Crutcher, and I) do at the Boothbay Literacy Retreat (Heinemann sponsored), Kylene calls the extra day there a *Lagniappe* session. It means "a little extra." In New Orleans the term means a little something extra a merchant gives you when you buy some merchandise. Think of this information as "a little extra," something beyond the quickwrite that might be useful to you and your students.

Introduction

༘

One line of a poem, the poet said—only one line, but thank God for that one line—drops from the ceiling . . . and you tap in the others around it with a jeweler's hammer.

—Annie Dillard, *The Writing Life*

Write fast—write badly—so you will write what you don't yet know you knew, and so you will outrun the censor within us all.

—Donald M. Murray, Pulitzer Prize-winning author

Never hesitate to imitate another writer. Imitation is part of the creative process for anyone learning an art or a craft. Bach and Picasso didn't spring full-blown as Bach or Picasso; they needed models. This is especially true of writing.

—William Zinsser

The simple rhythm of copying someone else's words gets us into the rhythm (of writing), then you begin to feel your own words.

—William Forrester, *Finding Forrester*

Because, for one thing, becoming a better writer is going to help you become a better reader, and that is the real payoff.

—Anne LaMott, *Bird by Bird*

Doing a quickwrite is like riding the wave of someone else's words until you find your own.

—Ralph Fletcher, classroom visit, 2015

Several times a week, at the beginning of class, I project a short piece (*most of the time* no more than one page) of writing on the whiteboard, read it out loud, and ask students to do a quickwrite in response. This writing is done in the response section of their writer's-reader's notebooks. The results of this simple routine are astounding. Consider the following example, written by Lindsay O. after I read aloud Cynthia Rylant's picture book *When I Was Young in the Mountains*.

Remembrance
For My Grandmother
Clarice Smith Chapman, 1914–1989
by Lindsay O.

I remember . . . we collected wild strawberries

And made mud pies and built

Block houses and guided

Our cart down the supermarket aisle

And picked carrots and washed

Dishes and baked cookies and cut

Paper dolls and watched chickadees

And played checkers and ate scrambled eggs and

Took our time on the stairs

And you never told me you were dying.

I wanted the chance to say goodbye.

In two to three minutes look what Lindsay was able to do: find a focus, bring the relationship with her grandmother to life with such specific details of all they did together, use the stylistic device of linking everything together with *and* to emphasize how well she remembered everything and how much these things meant to her, and capture surprise for the reader at the end with this turn—the turn by which she herself was surprised.

Poignant and powerful, but not so exceptional that other students can't do just as well. I've found that inviting students to write off a found idea or borrowed line for just two to three minutes produces good writing—often *really* good writing. Students are always surprised by the thinking that spills onto the page. I used to be; I'm not anymore. (I now use Lindsay's poem as a model for quickwrites, to stimulate the thinking and writing of other students; it's included in this collection on page 89.)

I have also found that helping students find a way to get their initial ideas on paper helps them build the confidence to realize they do have something to say. When the writing is so focused, so detailed, and so poignant so quickly, it gives them a solid direction for expanding on that idea.

Objective of This Book

The major objective of this book is to put a collection of writing that offers compelling models for quickwrites in the hands of teachers. These models are accessible, valuable, and meaningful invitations to writers, but they are only the beginning. As teachers, we have to find ways of helping students expand and build on these initial ideas so that they will *want* to write and, therefore, *will* write and read. It is through the actual process of developing writing that students learn to write. First, though, they need to get those initial ideas onto paper. Our written and oral responses to students in conferences as they write, and through craft lessons as they draft, help them build on these nuggets of possibilities. Quickwrites are one way to generate these nuggets.

What Is a Quickwrite?

A *quickwrite* is a first draft response to a short piece of writing, usually no more than one page of poetry or prose, a drawing, an excerpt from a novel or a short picture book. Since I did my first collection of quickwrites (Rief 2003), I have seen lots of prompts labeled as quickwrites, or freewriting exercises that last five to ten minutes, also labeled as quickwrites. That is not how I define the term.

I want students to write fast, but I want them to see an example of how someone else took an idea to the completion of a finished product. A mentor text. This is the indirect message I give the students each time I put a piece of writing in front of them for a quickwrite. I want the writing they are seeing and hearing to push them into their own ideas, either as a whole or through borrowing a line— any line—and writing from that line, even if that line sends them meandering in a completely different direction. This is writing to find writing, but using someone else's words to stimulate their thinking. Ralph Fletcher defines what I am asking students to do (I had three of his four sons in my eighth-grade language arts class) as "riding the wave of someone else's words," until you find your own. I love that image—riding a surfboard of words again and again until you find your own way of pushing yourself up, toes gripping, knees bent, body centered to stay on and ride that board with your own words, in your own style.

Kathryn Harrison, a novelist and memoirist, recently said in *The Atlantic* (Fassler 2016) that

> Writing is a process that demands cerebral effort, but it's also
> one informed by the unconscious. . . . I teach writing, and before

I taught I never would have guessed the thing I say most often is: "Please stop thinking." But people really write better without thinking, by which I mean without self-consciousness. I'm not calculating about what I write, which means I have very little control over it. It's not that I decide what to write and carry it out. It's more that I grope my way towards something—not even knowing what it is until I've arrived. . . . Of course, the intellect wants to kick in—and, in the later drafts it should.

Writing a first draft you can become paralyzed (with critical voices in your head). . . . I don't sit there waiting for that perfect, beautiful sentence, because I know I'm going to sit there forever. So, as I tell students—start out by tripping, why don't you? Then get up and fall over again. Just as long as you go.

This is what quickwrites do: allow us to write fast without censoring—it's what the subconscious allows us to say. We are surprised to realize we didn't know we knew what we knew until we wrote it down. With quickwrites I am asking students to grope and trip their way into finding what really matters to them.

To do a quickwrite, students and teacher write for two to three minutes off a found idea or borrowed line from a text, responding to something that sparks a reaction in the mind of the reader/listener. This process helps writers generate ideas and get words on paper. When I have students do a quickwrite, I specifically ask them to do the following:

- Write as quickly as they can for two to three minutes, capturing anything that comes to mind in response to the work as a whole.

- Borrow a line or part of a line (one of their own choosing or a particular line that I might suggest) from the work and write off, or from, that line nonstop for two to three minutes.

- Use a specific line or particular style as a model from which to write, as in the example of suggestions for Lindsay's poem, "Remembrance: For My Grandmother, Clarice Smith Chapman" (see page 89).

Paula Bourque, a teacher in Maine, describes the value of quickwrites this way:

In this high-stakes world of educational achievement students need opportunities to flex their creative and reflective thinking muscles without risk and judgment in order to discover more about themselves, their thinking, and their world. Given the ever-constraining limits of time on our teaching day this can be difficult to achieve. Quickwrites, microbursts of writing that are daily, short, and ungraded pieces of writing, can allow for that.

For years I watched many students staring into space, claiming they were "brainstorming" or they had nothing to write about. Just telling them to "write anything" didn't help; they already couldn't think of "anything." Quickwrites stimulate their thinking so that they can find words. Joel, an eighth grader, told me one day, "The quickwrites help me write down some things I didn't remember I knew. When I see them it makes me *want* to write, so I *do* write."

I can't work in a void, and neither can students. Quickwrites help them find words for their ideas in a concrete way. Once students have words on paper, I can help them develop those thoughts into effective, compelling pieces of writing. Quickwrites help all of us get out of the void. The main purpose of doing a quickwrite is simply to get words and ideas on paper.

The Benefits of Quickwrites

Writing and teaching writing can be intimidating. It is hard work, and it takes time. Quickwrites offer an easy and manageable writing experience that helps both students and teachers find their voices and develop their confidence, as they discover they have important things to say. This quick exercise pulls words out of the writer's mind. I am always surprised at the precision of language, level of depth and detail, and clarity of focus I hear when a student reads a three-minute quickwrite out loud. When the models for quickwrites are compelling and carefully chosen, students are able to focus closely and write clearly.

I do want to mention that I still have students who stare at me, stare at the blank page, stare at their pen as they roll it back and forth between their fingers, and write nothing. If they continually tell me they have nothing to say even by borrowing a line, or nothing to say even when I kneel beside them and ask them to talk to me about their thinking, I ask them, no, *tell them*—as a last resort—to copy the poem or the first few paragraphs of the essay into their writer's-reader's notebooks. They cannot sit, just staring into space. They must put words on paper. Ultimately, *in most cases*, they find their own words as they write the words of the text that sits in front of them.

Of course I have kids who really struggle getting their thinking on paper, even with a line in front of them to stimulate their thinking. I kneel next to those students, asking them to tell me what they are thinking, letting them talk it out first. Sometimes I jot down what they tell me to show them they do have ideas. They do have words. The first time I did this for Matt—he was talking, I was writing what he said—I asked him to read what I wrote out loud. He did, then said, "You are such a good writer." I laughed and said, "Those are *your* words, exactly what you said. *You* are such a good writer." Sometimes we have to do that several times to convince those kids that they have good ideas.

Over the years of using these invitations to write with students in my classroom and with teachers in workshops and courses, I've discovered so many of their benefits.

Quickwrites bring out the writer. They:

- give students ideas and frames for their own writing so they are not working in a void

- help students build a volume of writing from which to draw ideas for more extensive and developed pieces

- focus students' attention and stimulate their thinking at the beginning of a class

- provide and capture the nuggets of ideas for more expanded pieces

- encourage writing about important ideas, chosen to make us think and feel as we learn

- give students choices about what they write, how they write, and what works and does not work in a low-stakes situation

- are ungraded, allowing students to be creative, imaginative and reflective in their thinking

- help students focus on one subject in greater detail by giving them examples filled with sensory detail

- introduce students to a variety of stylistic devices and craft moves they might try in their writing.

Quickwrites build students' confidence. They:

- offer surprise when students discover that they didn't realize how much they know, or what they are thinking, until they begin writing

- allow kids to take risks in a nonthreatening, informal situation

- build confidence when students see the quality of their writing

- make writing accessible to all students, even those who struggle the most with words and ideas, because quickwrites are short, quick, nonthreatening, and directed toward a specific task.

Quickwrites develop fluency by increasing volume. They:

- keep students writing several times a week

- keep students writing beyond the quickwrite when they find themselves committed to a topic that matters to them

- offer ongoing practice for writing in sensible, realistic, and meaningful ways on demand or in timed situations.

Quickwrites bring out the reader. They:

- teach students to become better readers as they hear, see, and craft language

- teach students critical reading as they choose significant lines, and then draft and reconsider their ideas in the clearest ways

- provide examples of fine, compelling writing from their peers, their teacher, and professional writers

- introduce students to a variety of writers: poets, essayists, and fiction and nonfiction writers.

Quickwrites help teachers grow as writers. They:

- allow us time to write for two to three minutes each class period

- help us find ideas for writing and our voices as writers

- clarify our understandings of the difficulty of the task we are asking students to do, because we're doing what we ask them to do.

A peripheral benefit of using quickwrites is that they enhance students' ability to cope with timed writing assignments on specific topics. I remind them to approach such assignments as they would a quickwrite and use the same process to develop, expand, revise, and edit their thinking as they take the writing to a best draft. They are better able to face such daunting, timed tasks precisely because their quickwrite practice has made them more fluent and proficient.

Teaching with Quickwrites

In my teaching, I always try to remember that:

- The more I want students to know how to do something well, the more often they should do it.
- We learn to read by reading and writing.
- We learn to write by writing and reading.
- A person can read without writing, but cannot write without reading.

Quickwrites support all four of these principles. Following are some practices I've developed around quickwrites to help students read and write successfully.

Engage Students in Writing

- Share any of the pieces of writing in this book or other pieces that you find are meaningful and compelling to your students.
- Let the students see the pieces by projecting them on a whiteboard.
- Read the piece aloud to the students so they can hear it (practice ahead of time so that you really know the writing well).
- Ask students to try writing or drawing quickly based on any of the "Try This . . ." ideas at the bottom of each page.
- Write or draw your own quickwrites with the students. (Every one of us can spare two to three minutes, especially when we realize the value of writing for ourselves and for our students.)
- If more than half of the students are still writing after two or three minutes, let them continue for another minute or two.
- Give students credit (Tom Romano calls it "good faith participation") for doing the quickwrites, considering this first-draft thinking part of their notebook or journal writing.

Engage Students in Reading

- Ask if anyone would like to read what he or she wrote.

- Thank volunteers for sharing and comment specifically on what they did well.

- If you do several quickwrites in one period or during the week, ask students to read what they wrote (during the day or at the end of the week) and star the quickwrite that surprises them the most or that they like the most. This gives them a focus for what they might go back to as they develop more extensive pieces from the quickwrite.

- Read your own quickwrites to the students (ones you don't like as well as ones you like), and frequently show them how you develop some of the ideas into fuller pieces.

Extend the Quickwrites

- Allow the students a choice in which quickwrites remain undeveloped and which matter enough to expand or craft further into finished pieces. (All writing does not necessarily begin with a quickwrite. This is only *one* of the ways where we find possibilities for more developed pieces.)

- Teach the students the craft of revision as you talk with them about their writing, whether it comes from quickwrites or other sources.

- Every few weeks ask students to go back into their writer's-reader's notebooks and find the quickwrites or any other thinking that surprised them or they want to say more about, indicating that this thinking could be developed into a more expanded piece. (This is easier if the quickwrites are all kept in some kind of writer's-reader's notebook.)

Extend This Collection

- Add your students' writing and your own writing to this collection.

- Add the writing of professionals that you especially like to this collection.

- If there are particular kinds of writing you would like students to become more adept at, find models you can use as quickwrites to help them craft that kind of writing (essays, persuasive pieces, informational pieces, poetry, description, etc.).

The Models

Pieces selected for quickwrites are best as complete works, not stand-alone phrases or three-word prompts. (There are times when I break my own rule. A passage from a novel that can stand alone to get students thinking about a particular issue, place, or feeling, or several powerful quotes from well-known sources that can be looked at together to offer opposing positions on a controversial issue, can also lead to some compelling writing.) Students need to see, most of the time, a whole piece that is thoughtfully and carefully crafted. The selections need to be practical (tied to the kind of writing you would like students to try), accessible (pieces you know the students can connect to), and provocative (stimulate thinking or feeling in the student). They need to see something that touched them intellectually, aesthetically, and/or emotionally. Adolescents are in the throes of immense physical, emotional, intellectual, and social growth. The pieces of writing we choose to share with them should be ones with which they can connect on many of these levels. The most valuable sources of quickwrites are short works that are:

- language rich
- strong on sensory imagery
- evocative of strong feelings
- thought-provoking
- relevant and compelling to adolescents' interests.

When carefully chosen, quickwrite models also demonstrate the craft lessons we want to teach students: careful organization, compelling leads and endings, effective word choice, unique ways of framing or presenting a piece of writing, strong nouns and verbs, stylistic devices or craft moves, even conventions of language—or breaking the rules when done with intent.

Thoughtfully selected, quickwrite models invite students into writing in a way that encourages critical reading as they commit their voices to paper and grow as writers. I use the writing of professionals, the writing of my former students, and my own writing to stimulate thinking for quickwrites. In her journal, Maggie, one of my eighth graders, wrote, "I had never done quickwrites before, and because of the limited time given I've found myself writing things I didn't know I knew or felt. They really help me get a sense of who I am and help me come up with ideas."

That is the power of a well-chosen quickwrite model.

About the Models in This Collection

I have assembled the pieces in this collection in a framework that underscores the way adolescents view themselves and in the schema in which I frame my curriculum for the year. Look through this book and arrange the way you present or use any of the writing within based on the way you frame your year.

Seeing Inward. How do students view themselves? What choices do they make as writers and readers that reflect those views?

Leaning Outward. What do students notice and understand when they step outside of themselves? What are the choices they notice that writers make in the books they are reading—not just about the topics, but the craft moves they make to engage a reader more fully?

Beyond Self. What do the students notice about the world at large as they choose more challenging topics and issues to both write and read about?

Looking Back. When students look back on some of the decisions and choices they've made in their lives, how does that reflective stance help them develop and grow into more articulate, thoughtful citizens of the world?

The pieces of writing I use for quickwrites come from my eighth-grade students (signified with their first name and last initial), from several teachers, and from my own writing and the writing of professionals. In addition to using the writing of numerous poets, I also use excerpts from novels. These short passages stimulate students' thinking about themselves in response to the passage, touch on the big ideas writers are developing in their novels, shed a light on some of the craft moves or techniques writers use to present their stories, and, ultimately, sell the students on the book, nudging them to read it on their own. I have included a list of the novels from which I most frequently draw passages at the end of this book.

There are endless configurations to use based on themes or issues or genres being explored in the classroom. The writing of scientists, historical figures, mathematicians, or musicians could be used in any discipline to immerse and focus students in the thinking in these fields.

This book also includes several sketches and drawings as possibilities for stimulating ideas. Over the years I have noticed that the students who struggle the most with words find a way to start writing if they first work with their ideas visually, because students craft pictures in the same way they would craft words—to clearly represent their thinking.

My goal is to help students grow and become the most articulate, literate young men and women they can be in the short time (fifty minutes per day) that I work with them.

How to Use These Models in the Classroom

Several times a week, I begin the class with one of these pieces—sometimes using them in the order in which they appear in the book, other times pulling pieces because they are related to the topic we may be studying (the Holocaust, other human rights or social justice issues, relationships, becoming a writer, etc.) or they lead us into thinking about a particular genre (personal essay, flash fiction, persuasion, etc.). I make sure the students can see the piece of writing, read it aloud so they can hear it, and then ask them to write silently for two to three minutes. I may ask students to choose one of the following ways to guide their writing—the ways that also shape the "Try This" suggestions on each page:

- Write as quickly and as specifically as you can for two to three minutes anything that this piece of writing or drawing brings to mind for you.

- Borrow a line and write as quickly and as specifically as you can, letting the line lead your thinking.

- Do something specific with the writing or with a particular line from the writing.

- *Ignore* anything I ask you to do if what you see and hear already has you writing.

Although I usually ask the students to respond to only one piece of writing, there are times when I might group two or three pieces together and ask the students to respond to one after another, or to the group as a whole.

The whole point is to get students writing—which gets them thinking, which gets them writing, which gets them reading and writing.

Writer's-Reader's Notebooks

My students do their quickwrites in the response section of the writer's-reader's notebook (Rief 2007), so that these ideas can be collected for future development into a more extended piece of writing, *if* students choose to do that. I've found that students need one place to continually collect ideas; otherwise, that writing on single sheets of paper gets tossed, buried in their lockers, or left in the classroom.

I want students to know that all of their writing matters. They need a volume of writing to find the best writing. I tell them the anecdote that Jane Kearns, one of my writing teachers at the University of New Hampshire, told us many years ago. What does it mean when a player on a professional baseball team is batting .350? Inevitably a student will say, "It means he's making a million bucks!" True. And what it really means is, he is only getting a successful hit 35 percent of the time. He strikes out, walks, or is thrown out 65 percent of the time. If a writer produces three pages of good writing out of ten pages, he's in the big leagues. A writer needs to step to the plate and put words on paper to find the strongest writing. Quickwrites help them produce that volume of writing from which to select the topics or issues that matter to them to develop into their best writing.

It also matters that they capture their thinking. Otherwise, it's lost. I can't remember what I was thinking last night, but if I have put it in my writer's-reader's notebook, it is there for me to find, and potentially use. Our students need to understand those same reasons for daily writing.

Keeping their writing in one writer's-reader's notebook also allows me to respond to their thinking regularly and easily. I read their notebooks every two weeks, affirming their thoughtfulness in their reading and writing. My response, although it may only be underlining something or jotting notes and questions, is meant to support their thinking and push them to grow as readers and writers. (Because I have close to one hundred students, I stagger the collection of these notebooks: one class on Monday, one on Tuesday, one on Wednesday, and one on Thursday—*every other week*. Almost without exception, I return their notebooks the next day.)

My eighth graders are expected to complete two to four pages of writing in their notebooks each week. This includes their quickwrites, their responses to books they are reading at night, their responses to short or long pieces we are reading together in class, and many of their first draft ideas for writing. Counting quickwrites toward their writing total lets students know how much I value this kind of writing and encourages them to value it also. It encourages them to treat it as fertile ground from which further writing and thinking may spring.

Taking Quickwrites Further

After writing, I invite students to share their work out loud to the entire class or in small groups at their tables. Sometimes many kids read what they wrote; other times, no one does. Sometimes I read my own quickwrite, and other times I might mention why I am not sharing what I wrote.

Occasionally I ask the students what they noticed about another student's writing that struck them or stayed with them. What did the writer do that made that writing so effective? What do they want to know more about? What are the questions they have for the writer? What else could the writer do to elaborate on that idea? I also remind students that if someone reads something that makes them think of something in their own lives, they should jot it down before it disappears.

These quickwrites are seeds of ideas, the beginning of a piece to be worked on right away or, at the very least, captured for later use. Students have the option to continue working from or on the quickwrite, to just let it sit in their notebooks for later development, or to never work on it again.

I frequently go back to a piece of writing a second or third time to look at the questions students might have had, to look at the language of the piece, or to talk about the craft of the writing. In several "Interludes" throughout the book, I have stopped to show you what a student did in response to a specific piece as he or she went from a quickwrite to a finished piece.

Interludes: Developing a Piece to Its Fullest Potential

Throughout the pages of this book, I have included numerous pieces of my students' writing, my writing, and several pieces by teachers with whom I have worked in courses or in professional development workshops—all sparked by a quickwrite. These examples are meant to illuminate the possibilities in your students, so they can see how a few bursts of writing can lead to more fully developed ideas. These interludes include notebook responses and/or best drafts of writing, all of which were begun as quickwrites.

How the students develop these initial ideas (the quickwrites) to their fullest potential (their best drafts) is the heart of writing. It does not happen seamlessly or quickly. But it is essential to the process of bettering the writing. It necessitates feedback from listeners. I want you and your students to see the potential and possibilities in their quickwrites. They are meant to spark ideas that can be developed through the following process.

My students receive response to their drafts from their peers as well as from me. It does not matter how many pieces of writing you are asking your students to take to a best draft. What matters is that each of those pieces receives feedback that helps the writer move his or her ideas forward.

Before I ask students to respond to each other's writing, I read a draft of my writing to them. I explain what I need the most help with. (I might need a more engaging lead, a better way of showing the passing of time, an ending that allows the reader to draw her own conclusions, or something as specific as, What does my use of fragments do to you as a reader?) I hand them each three sticky notes. On the three notes they write:

Liked/Heard Stayed with me

Questions

Suggestions

The structure helps the students stay focused on the writing they are listening to and offer the kinds of comments that will make the writing better. Listeners write the phrases, questions, and suggestions down as they are listening to the piece being read to them, so they don't forget what they were thinking. Sometimes it takes two readings: one so listeners get an overview of the writing, and a second so they can be more specific.

When writers are able to identify the area in which they need the most help, it often eliminates having to read the whole piece, especially if it is more than several pages long. These are content conferences—to make the meaning as clear as possible. This is why it is essential to have the writer read his writing to listeners instead of handing it to them. We have been conditioned to notice the problems with mechanics and tend to mention these things first. If the writer reads, the listener can't see the mistakes. Thus, the focus remains on the content.

Students always read their own writing in a conference when they are working to revise it. I want them to be responsible for hearing their own voices as they write, revise, and edit.

Repeating sections or phrases back to the writer tells her that she was heard, that the language or construction affected the listener in some way, and that these might be areas the writer wants to preserve. As I model this with my own writing, I put check marks next to these phrases or sections.

Questions suggest to writers the information that they might consider adding. Writers must ask themselves: Is it important to add that? How many listeners had the same questions? What questions seem relevant to answer? I model this thinking with my students' responses to my writing.

Listeners' suggestions should be focused on the areas the writer perceives as needing help. Did the writer want a stronger title? A more engaging lead? More detail for the character? More convincing arguments? Was the writer wondering about tense? Or point of view? Or change in time? Would this piece work better as poetry or prose?

This is the structure students must follow as they respond to each other, whether the writer is sharing with one person, a small group, or the whole class. It is the structure that best helps the writer make his writing better. Generic response—"That was good" or "That was interesting"—is no help at all.

Approximately half of the writing the students choose to take to a best draft comes from quickwrites. Showing your students the best drafts of some of my students helps them see the possibilities for extending their own quickwrites. What I hope they see with these interludes is that the directions these pieces take are never the same. The possibilities are endless, even though they all begin with response to the same mentor text. This gives students choices, even within a frame.

Relooking at the Models

Any one of the models, both quickwrites and interludes, included in this book can be looked at a second or third time to help the students gain insight about leads, endings, line breaks, use of punctuation, titles, layers of meaning, fragments, word choices, and so on. The possibilities for using the models to explore craft elements are virtually limitless. At the end of the introduction I have included a chart that could be used to help students develop a list of craft moves from the models in this book that might help them make their own writing stronger.

In the same way you model your own writing when soliciting feedback to that writing, give students some examples of what you notice in these models of writing to help them develop the habit of reading as writers, noticing what a writer does to craft his writing. Also essential to this insight is the ability to notice and describe what the craft move does to the writing and/or the reader.

Don Murray said again and again that good writing makes us think *or* feel something; the best writing makes us think *and* feel something. So many of the students whose writing is in this collection, as both quickwrites and interludes, didn't think they had anything to say. Giving them another student's words or the words of professionals to hold onto, until they found their own, gave them the confidence to know they could show us what they think *and* feel.

Invitations to Writing

This book is a series of invitations to students and teachers, intended to help them find ideas for writing. It does not attempt to oversimplify a complex process. Quickwrites offer beginnings, support, connections, and encouragement in a practical, concrete, accessible, and provocative way. They help students realize they do have something to say, and that they are capable of saying those things in a way that engages readers.

Adolescents are often uncomfortable and insecure about writing. Quickwrites are nonthreatening precisely because they are short and quick, yet focused. They provide accessible entry into significant matters because they are chosen for their compelling topics, well-crafted language, and unique styles. When carefully selected so that students can readily relate to them, they give students models that stimulate their thinking about their own topics in concrete, specific ways. As they experiment and craft their ideas, observations, beliefs, knowledge, and opinions, students develop into critical readers and thinkers. They also develop as human beings, answering their biggest questions: *Who am I? Where do I fit in this world?*

Kira, a language arts teacher who was a student in a course I was teaching at the University of New Hampshire, literally came running to me at the beginning of the third class, breathless. "You know how I told you I hate writing and was petrified about teaching it and that I had nothing to say and no matter what you did I knew it wouldn't help me but I can't believe what I've done with these quickwrites and I was so excited I've been working with my kids all week and I've written things I didn't know I knew and they've written things they didn't know

they knew and every day I can't wait to work on this writing and neither can they and I can't believe their writing can be this good."

And the writing *is* good. There is something about asking students to write quickly and for a short period of time, with good examples in front of them, that leads them to think in detailed, explicit, focused ways that are imaginative, creative, and unique. They say things they didn't know they were going to say. They are allowing themselves the opportunity to engage in cognitive surprise.

Leading Students to Literacy

Don Graves often said to me that "democracies are dependent on the quality of their citizens' thinking. . . . And one of the best ways to develop solid thinkers early on is by asking children to think clearly through a written text."

In our attempts as a nation to lead our children to literacy, we have nearly abandoned writing—writing for real reasons, for real audiences. I believed this twenty years ago and still believe it is true today—unfortunately. I think we have also forgotten that a person can read without writing, but he or she cannot write without reading. If we neglect writing while focusing our attention almost exclusively on reading, it is also *at the expense of reading.*

What has happened to the writing that used to flourish in classrooms? Have we forgotten, ignored, or—even worse—abandoned it? Have we dismissed long-term, real writing while focusing all our attention on one-word answers or formulaic paragraphs to standardized, shortened passages of reading, supposedly to determine our students' critical reading skills?

Have we forgotten that *writing is thinking*? When students write, they are engaged in a recursive process of critical thinking: Have I said clearly what I want to say? Are my thoughts well organized and clearly developed? Have I used the sharpest, tightest, most vivid language? Does my lead capture readers and give them a clear direction and focus? Does my writing make the reader think, or feel, or learn something?

When students are engaged in the process of writing something that matters to them, they do write and they do read, thoughtfully and thoroughly.

Our goals should be loftier than raising reading scores or raising writing scores. Our classrooms should be laboratories of high-level thinking where the activities stimulate our students' curiosity and imagination, where the students are the problem solvers, the thinkers. It is through speaking, reading, *and writing* that our students become articulate, literate, confident, and thoughtful citizens of the world.

Quickwrites get students thinking.

Seeing Inward

Rambling Autobiography
by Linda Rief

© 2018 by Linda Rief from *The Quickwrite Handbook: 100 Mentor Texts to Jumpstart Your Students' Thinking and Writing.* Portsmouth, NH: Heinemann.

TRY THIS (as quickly and as specifically as you can for 2–3 minutes)

+ Write your own "rambling autobiography." Let each new phrase take you in any direction.

+ If one phrase tends to send you in a direction about one topic, jot down all that comes to mind.

+ If you are stuck, and not yet putting words to paper, start with one of the phrases in my piece: "I was born at . . . I have lied to . . . One of my friends once said . . ." Change anything to make it yours.

I was born at the height of World War II just as Anne Frank was forced into Bergen-Belsen by the Nazis. I adore Brigham's vanilla ice cream in a sugar cone and dipped in chocolate jimmies. October is my favorite month, when the air turns green pear crisp. I roll down the car window and listen to the maples turn apple red and the oaks pumpkin orange. I bought my favorite jacket for a dime at the Methodist Church rummage sale. I have lied to my parents. With four high school friends I cut down a tree in the town forest for our Holiday Dance. I didn't know until the police arrived at the high school that each tree had been dedicated to a WW II veteran. I never read a book for pleasure until I was 38 years old. One of my students once leaned in to me in an interview and said, "My mother's having a baby; this is the one she wants." When I was 12 I set the organdy curtains in our bathroom on fire, playing with matches. My not-so-secret place to hide was high in the maple tree in our front yard where I could spy on neighbors. I can still smell wet white sheets pulled through the ringer washer when I think of Grammy Mac. I dated Edmundo in high school because it angered my father. I fainted when I heard the sound of the zipper as the mortician closed the body bag holding my mother. I gave birth to twin sons. I once had dinner with Judy Blume. I am a teacher who writes. I want to be a writer who teaches.

TEACHER NOTE Notice that each phrase could be developed into a more extended piece. Your students' rambling autobiographies will also be filled with possibilities. Saying "Tell me more about _____" helps them develop those ideas.

On Being Asked to Select the Most Memorable Day of My Life

by Rebecca K.

Five-thousand thirty-seven. That's how many days I have to choose from. How could I just pick one that's my most memorable?

The day I turned ten? The day my brother, dad, and I hiked Mt. Washington? The day I rode my first horse? The day I won my first blue ribbon with him? The day I first met my youngest brother? The day I won the Young Naturalist Award? The day I finally learned how to do a parallel turn in skiing? The day I first held my boxer puppy?

But I don't remember the days. I remember the moments. I don't remember the day I turned ten. I remember eleven pink candles on a chocolate cake, one for good luck. I don't remember the day I won my first blue ribbon with my horse. I just remember the feel of that last jump, how the world seemed to hold still and we were in the air for too long not to be flying. I remember the buttercups I had wound into his braided mane. I don't remember the day I finally learned how to parallel ski. I just remember the second when everything came together and I was suddenly gliding down over the bright, white snow that was making rainbows dance off my skis.

I don't remember whole days. Just moments, that I can't give a date or time. When I was little I tried to capture the brilliant light of stained glass windows in my hand and carry it home. Moments are like that; I can't hold them, but I still remember them.

TRY THIS (as quickly and as specifically as you can for 2–3 minutes)

+ Write down all that happened on the most memorable day in your life.

+ Write down anything that Rebecca's words bring to mind for you.

+ Think of one or several of those memorable moments that linger with you. Start by framing them as questions, the way Rebecca did.

+ Once you have jotted down as many memorable moments as possible, choose one to describe in greater detail. What are the sights, sounds, smells, and feelings associated with that memory?

On my own time, I take some of my quickwrites to a more developed piece. Other times, that writing just sits in my writer's-reader's notebook until I can use it. In response to Rebecca's piece, I wrote the following:

Most Memorable Days
by Linda Rief

How many days do I have to choose from? Twenty-three thousand, three hundred, and sixty. Which one of these days is the most memorable?

The day I held our first grandchild in the palm of my hand? The day I received my driver's license? The day dad let me take the Buick for the first time by myself? The day I saw our twin sons? The day I learned George's submarine had hit something on the ocean floor and there was no word of their condition? The day I heard President Kennedy had been assassinated? Or planes had smashed into the World Trade Centers in New York City? The day I learned my mom had colon cancer? The day I figured out my dad was an alcoholic? The day I tried to convince him to check himself into Bridgewater State Hospital? The day my first book arrived in the mail? The day I met Miep Gies, the woman who risked her life by taking care of Anne Frank's family for two years, while they hid in that attic annex in Amsterdam, because "it was the right thing to do."

I'm not sure how I will use this writing. But I have captured my thinking for the moment. What I notice is that each question carries its own story. I have so many possibilities from which to build, if and when I choose to do so.

© 2018 by Linda Rief from The Quickwrite Handbook: 100 Mentor Texts to Jumpstart Your Students' Thinking and Writing. Portsmouth, NH: Heinemann.

TEACHER NOTE Keeping a writer's-reader's notebook as teachers and doing the quickwrites ourselves shows our students we value all we are asking them to do. We have little time to write, but we can take two to three minutes to write with our students. (Each time I read Rebecca's piece to each of my classes, I added more to my initial quickwrite.)

Excerpt from *The Running Dream*
by Wendelin Van Draanen

I AM A RUNNER.

That's what I do.

That's who I am.

Running is all I know, or want, or care about.

It was a race around the soccer field in third grade that swept me into a real love of running.

Breathing the sweet smell of spring grass.

Sailing over dots of blooming clover.

Beating all the boys.

After that, I couldn't stop. I ran everywhere. Raced everyone.

I loved the wind across my cheeks, through my hair.

Running aired out my soul.

It made me feel *alive*.

And now?

I'm stuck in this bed, knowing I'll never run again.

TRY THIS (as quickly and as specifically as you can for 2–3 minutes)

+ Write out anything this excerpt brings to mind for you.

+ Think about something you are passionate about (something that "airs out your soul," "makes you feel alive") and write down everything that makes this activity so important to you.

+ Start with the line "I AM A _____" and fill in the blank, describing all that you do, think, feel, experience while doing this activity.

+ Change the line to "I am not a _____," expanding on all the reasons why you are not.

+ Her last two lines say she will never run again. What has stopped you from doing something you love doing?

TEACHER NOTE Notice the short, clipped sentences along with longer ones that give a cadence, or rhythm, to the piece, the way a runner might be getting into the rhythm of running and breathing. You could use this piece when looking at craft moves—especially length of sentences and layout on the page—and all they do for the reader.

© 2018 by Linda Rief from *The Quickwrite Handbook: 100 Mentor Texts to Jumpstart Your Students' Thinking and Writing.* Portsmouth, NH: Heinemann.

TRY THIS (as quickly and as specifically as you can for 2–3 minutes)

+ Think of a place that you love (a mountain or lake cabin, a tree house, a perch in an oak tree, a tree stand, the roof of an apartment building, the baseball dugout, the stage for a performance, a fort, a concert, a boat in the middle of the ocean, etc.) and describe all that you see, hear, smell, touch, taste, and do there. What makes this place so special?

+ Take an opposite stance and think of a place you dislike (a locker room, a five-hour car ride squished in the back seat with your siblings, the dentist's chair, the principal's office, the school cafeteria, etc.). What do you see, hear, smell, touch, taste, and do there?

+ Borrow Rylant's line "When I was young in the . . ." (or "at the . . .") and write down all that comes to mind about that place you love or that place you dislike.

When I Was Young at the Ocean
by Linda Rief

With thanks to Cynthia Rylant for When I Was Young in the Mountains

When I was young at the ocean, I sat at the edge of the wooden pier and dangled my toes in the water. Like tiny rowboats my toes skimmed the rolling waves, ever alert for sharks. Sometimes I sat cross-legged in shorts and tee-shirt, a bamboo fishing pole stretched to catch mackerel. No one ever told me to bait the hook.

When I was young at the ocean, I cracked open mussels and periwinkles and clams, and ran my fingers across their gushy insides. I squished seaweed nodules between my forefinger and thumb, anxious for the pop and spray from the moist insides.

When I was young at the ocean, I burned my shoulders and smelled of Noxzema through the entire month of July. I drank in the aroma of hip roses, salt water, and seaweed. At low tide I played croquet with the Queen of Hearts, flew to the moon in a hammock, and fed my dolls deviled ham sandwiches in the shade of the screened house.

As the tide came in, water lapped at the rocky shore. The skin of my feet toughened as I paced those rounded stones, my eyes searching for skippers. *When I was young, I never wished* to climb the mountains, or live in the city, or camp in the forest. The ocean was enough. It still is.

TEACHER NOTE After reading this to students, you might point out the writer's use of italics in that first line and ending lines as a way of showing she borrowed that line directly from Rylant's picture book, changing only *mountains* to *ocean*. You might also point out the repetition of the line "When I was young at the ocean," and ask them what the repetition does for them as a reader. (As the writer, the use of repetition pushes me back into those memories.)

Excerpt from *The Terrible Two*
by Mac Barnett and Jory John

On your first day at a new school in a new town, you got to decide what kind of kid you were going to be. You could be the smart kid, or the kid who has cool shoes. You could be the kid who knows everything about old cars, or current events, or World War I. The kid who always has ChapStick. Chess kid, basketball kid, student-government kid. Kid who organizes canned-food drives. Front-row kid. Back-row kid. Kid who always has his hand up even though he doesn't know the answers. Kid who's allowed to see R-rated movies. Kid who isn't allowed to see R-rated movies but says he does and just makes up their plots based on the previews. Kid whose family doesn't own a TV and just wants to watch your TV. On the first day of school you could fake a French accent and be the foreign kid. You could bring your teacher a gift and be the kiss-up kid. Expensive-school-supplies kid. Kid who sharpens his pencil ten times per period. The two-different-socks quirky kid. The kid who wears shorts every day regardless of the weather. Today was the day when you could decide to become a new kid and be that kid for the rest of your life.

TRY THIS (as specifically and as quickly as you can for 2–3 minutes)

+ Write out anything this excerpt brings to mind for you.

+ Borrow any line, letting the line lead your thinking.

+ Use the line "I'm the kind of kid who . . ." and write out who you are as that kind of kid.

© 2018 by Linda Rief from *The Quickwrite Handbook: 100 Mentor Texts to Jumpstart Your Students' Thinking and Writing*. Portsmouth, NH: Heinemann.

TRY THIS (as quickly and as specifically as you can for 2–3 minutes)

+ Write out all that Kevin's words bring to mind for you.

+ Borrow any line, letting the line lead your thinking as you write.

+ Describe the thing that you've been trying to "get right" in your life. Describe the frustration and the success you've experienced. (It might be accomplishing a particular move in a sport, finally learning how to play a certain song, trying to get along with a parent or sibling, or something personal that you've struggled with, such as Kevin's stutter, anger, or some other emotion.) What have you been trying to "get right"?

Getting It Right
by Kevin Carey

In grammar school I stuttered,
felt the hot panic on my face
when my turn to read crept up the row.
Even when I counted the paragraphs
and memorized the passage,
I'd trip on the first or second word,
and then it would be over,
the awful hesitation, the word
clinging to the lining of my throat
rising only too late to avoid
the laughter around me. I was never
the smartest kid in the room,
but I had answers I knew were right
yet was afraid to say them.
Years later it all came out, flowing
sentences I practiced over and over,
Shakespeare or Frost, my own tall tales
in low-lit barrooms, scribbled
in black-bound journals, rehearsing,
anticipating my turn, my time,
a way of finally getting it right.

© 2018 by Linda Rief from *The Quickwrite Handbook: 100 Mentor Texts to Jumpstart Your Students' Thinking and Writing*. Portsmouth, NH: Heinemann.

Notice what Lucas S. did to take his writing beyond a quickwrite.

After an especially difficult episode at speech therapy, Lucas confided his frustration to his brother Devin. In response to Kevin Carey's poem, he had written the words of his brother to him in his writer's-reader's notebook— "Imagine your brain full of tons of wires."

When we talked about memoir over the next few weeks, those were the words Lucas went back to as the basis, and lead, to develop into a more complete piece. This is the reason why quickwrites are so important—the chance to capture a few lines of something important that pops into your head from the stimulus of someone else's writing. This is also the reason why maintaining a writer's-reader's notebook is so important—a place to capture that thinking for looking at again and again.

Floating Words
by Lucas S.

"Imagine your brain full of tons of wires," my older brother explained as we were falling asleep. "And those wires are covered in protection, like plastic. That is myelin." I nodded in the dark, not quite understanding, but concentrating hard to picture wires snaking around inside my five-year-old head. "Your protective coating got a little messed up, which makes some of the messages traveling along the wires leak out, getting lost."

I envisioned a word leaking out and floating lost in my brain, like an escaped balloon drifting up into space. I imagined searching desperately for that lost balloon floating in the vast sky, powerless to bring it back. I thought of all the times I wanted to say one word but another, similar-sounding one finally popped out of my mouth; times I'd end up trying to mime a word; times I'd just give up and mumble, "Never mind." Finally, I understood why I had been going to speech therapy four times a week for as long as I could remember.

Invariably, wooden flavored sticks began my thirty-minute sessions. The grey-haired therapist assured me they helped place my tongue in the right place.

continues

Interlude

continued from previous page

All I knew is that they made me gag, and the grape flavor tasted more like medicine than fruit. But I smiled and tried my best sitting on a little wooden chair, and looked forward to my lollipop. Sometimes the lollipops ran out, and all they had was a basket of stickers. Those days left me with the nasty grape taste on the roof of my mouth.

After I understood why I had to endure those visits, I still didn't find my words any faster. But I did become even more determined to make myself understood. I'd been expressing myself through symbols ever since I was a toddler, using sign language to avoid frustration. Three more years of therapy would pass before I found a new way to communicate.

I remember that first time I picked up an old video camera and made a short film featuring my fat cat, Tobey. The camera showed the story better than I could have told it aloud. My audience cheered and gave me two thumbs up, and no one asked me to explain a single moment. I had stumbled on the perfect way to tell my stories to the world without worrying about those pesky leaky wires.

At first, my films were action-packed Lego Star Wars movies with more battles than dialogue. Later, I turned my camera to spoofs and recruited my neighbors and brothers to star in a series featuring Dora the Explorer. First, my film landed Dora in the midst of World War II. Next, she visited the underworld. And, finally, Dora went to boot camp. My films were interrupted with silly ads and infomercials.

After seeing Ken Burns speak at UNH, I turned to documentaries. My brothers and I teamed up to show what our family had done to make our home more sustainable and ended up winning an award from New Hampshire Public Television. I won two more awards and was invited to film an international water expert, Maude Barlow, at a speech in Durham. Several of my recent films have even aired on local television.

A miniature Oscar sits on my bureau awaiting the real Oscar to be added to the collection. Runaway balloons no longer haunt me. It seems that holding a video camera was the secret to helping me grasp those floating words. Now, the only balloons in my mind are the ones that will decorate my party after the Academy Awards.

© 2018 by Linda Rief from *The Quickwrite Handbook: 100 Mentor Texts to Jumpstart Your Students' Thinking and Writing*. Portsmouth, NH: Heinemann.

TEACHER NOTE The description of how Lucas' piece of writing began with his brother's words to him after he had written about speech therapy and trying to "get his words right" in response to Carey's poem is worth showing your students. A piece of writing often develops over time—finding a line or two about something that matters and getting feedback to better the ideas. (See "Interludes: Developing a Piece to Its Fullest Potential" in the Introduction.)

When She Was Fifteen
by Linda Rief

© 2018 by Linda Rief from *The Quickwrite Handbook: 100 Mentor Texts to Jumpstart Your Students' Thinking and Writing*. Portsmouth, NH: Heinemann.

When she was fifteen she believed the world would be destroyed by an atomic bomb but Debbie and Pam would probably live because their fathers were rich and they had bomb shelters. She believed the most important thing in life was a date for the Junior Prom, but she'd never have one because her nose was too long, her hair was too short, her legs were too fat, and she wasn't a cheerleader. She believed David loved Paula because Paula plucked her eyebrows.

She believed she was poor because her family had a linoleum floor in the living-room and only one bathroom. There was no Maytag washer or dryer at her house. Not even a Kenmore. When she was sixteen and in charge of laundry, she drove to the laundromat in Quincy, two towns away, where no one she knew could see her wash and fold her underwear in public.

Summers she worked two jobs. Days she pitched whiffle balls to five-year-olds and colored clowns from picnic benches. She made gimp bracelets and wove real Indian change purses for little kids who had no money and saved only sticks and shells and rocks. She awarded blue ribbons and red ribbons and white ribbons for jumping the highest, running the farthest, and crying the least. At night she filled Dixie cups with butterscotch sundaes floating in marshmallow. She poured strawberry frappes and chocolate milk shakes from The Fountain at Paragon Park, while the roller coaster screamed overhead with flailing arms, the gypsy lied, and the fat lady bragged about the two-headed calf.

Weekends she watched Babe Ruth baseball from behind the chain link fence at the high school. David at first, Charlie at second, and Mac at catcher. While their parents clapped and girlfriends cheered, she dated Edmundo because he was Puerto Rican and Jesse because he was black, but mostly because it angered her father.

TRY THIS (as quickly and as specifically as you can for 2–3 minutes)

+ Start with the line, "When I was _____ (any age) I believed . . ." and write all you believed at that age.

+ Write out anything this brings to mind for you, thinking specifically of the sights, sounds, smells, tastes, and touch associated with those beliefs, happenings, or people.

+ Change the third-person pronoun *she* to *I* or *he* or *you* and write down all that comes to mind when you change the pronoun. Let the writing take you where it wants to go, even if it is not the happening truth.

© 2018 by Linda Rief from *The Quickwrite Handbook: 100 Mentor Texts to Jumpstart Your Students' Thinking and Writing*. Portsmouth, NH: Heinemann.

TRY THIS (as quickly and as specifically as you can for 2–3 minutes)

✦ Write out anything this excerpt brings to mind for you.

✦ Think about an activity you do that also has "Rigor Mortis Bend," the place where you have to push yourself to complete the activity. It could be the competition of any sport, that last lap in the 400-meter relay in swimming when your arms feel like jelly. It could be hunting, the moment in that tree stand or in that blind when you know you cannot move, no matter how long it takes, to keep the animal from running. Write out all you do, feel, think, or notice at that moment.

✦ Van Draanen's last line implies that something besides the character's running is causing her to feel this same way. Write out something you've experienced that makes you feel like you are living on "Rigor Mortis Bend," a time that something you have to do seems so hard you think you can't make it or can't do it, but you have to.

Excerpt from *The Running Dream*
by Wendelin Van Draanen

RIGOR MORTIS BEND

It's a place in the 400-meter race where every cell of your body locks up.

Your lungs ache for air.

Your quads turn to cement.

Your arms pump desperately, but they're stiff and feel like lead.

Rigor Mortis Bend is the last turn of any track, and at Liberty High you're greeted with a headwind.

The finish line comes into view and you will yourself toward it, but the wind pushes you back, your body begs you to give up, and the whole world seems to grind into slow motion.

Your determination is all that's left.

It forces your muscles to fire.

Forces you to stay in the race.

Forces you to survive the pain of this moment.

Your teammates scream for you to push.

Push! Push! Push!

You can do it!

But their voices are muffled by the gasping for air, the pounding of earth, the pumping of blood, the need to collapse.

I feel like I'm living on Rigor Mortis Bend.

Excerpt from *All American Boys*
by Jason Reynolds and Brendan Kiely

Dad was all about discipline and believed that if you work hard, good things happen to you no matter what. Of course, part of working hard, to him, was looking the part, dressing the part, and speaking the part, which Spoony didn't really vibe with.

Spoony had, I don't know, maybe eight or nine locs sprouting from his head like antennae. Thick and matted like strips of carpet, but I always thought they looked pretty cool. Dad . . . not so much. They'll think you're doing drugs, he'd say. Spoony's clothes were always two (or three or four) sizes too big. That was just his style. That was pretty much his whole generation's style. Nineties hip-hop, gritty, realness. Wu-Tang. Biggie. Hoodies and unlaced boots. They'll think you're selling drugs, Dad would say. Why can't you get a haircut? Why can't you dress like a respectable adult? Why can't you set an example for your brother? Huh, son? Why? And because Spoony was tired of explaining himself, and Dad was asking him to change, they kept their conversations short and sweet. Like Spoony greeting him, "Dad," head nod. Followed by Dad saying, "Spoony," head nod. And that was that.

© 2018 by Linda Rief from *The Quickwrite Handbook: 100 Mentor Texts to Jumpstart Your Students' Thinking and Writing*. Portsmouth, NH: Heinemann.

TRY THIS (as quickly and as specifically as you can for 2–3 minutes)

- Write out anything this excerpt brings to mind for you.

- Describe a time you felt compelled to tell the truth—about a book or anything else.

- In your history as a reader, what does this particular excerpt bring to mind in your own experience?

- In what ways has any book you've read, or one that has been read to you, been a bit of a disappointment? Or, how was it the best book you ever read?

Excerpt from *Counting by 7s*
by Holly Goldberg Sloan

Mrs. King had just plowed her way through a popular picture book. It featured the hallmarks of most pre-school literature: repetition, some kind of annoying rhyming, and bold-faced scientific lies.

I remember Mrs. King asking the class: "How does this book make you feel?"

The appropriate answer as far as she was concerned was "tired," because the overly cheery instructor forced us to lie down on sticky rubber mats for twenty minutes after "lunchtime picture book."

. . . while my classmates dozed off, I obsessively worried about the hygiene of the linoleum floor.

. . . I recall looking around at my fellow inmates, thinking: *Would someone, anyone, just shout out the word* tired?

. . . after days of hearing more lies from an adult than I'd been exposed to in my whole lifetime—everything from how fairies cleaned up the classroom at night to insane explanations for earthquake preparedness kits—I was at some kind of breaking point.

So when the teacher specifically said: "Willow, how does this book make *you* feel?" I had to tell the truth:

"It makes me feel really bad. The moon can't hear someone say good night; it is two hundred thirty-five thousand miles away. And bunnies don't live in houses. Also, I don't think the artwork is very interesting."

"But really, hearing you read the book makes me feel bad mostly because I know it means you are going to make us all lie down on the floor—and germs there could make us sick. There's a thing called salmonella and it is very dangerous. Especially to kids."

That afternoon, I learned the word *weirdo* because that's what I was called by the other kids.

Fifteen
by Annika B.

Fourteen had just become familiar.

I stopped stumbling, stuttering over the word,

Hoping it was right,

Knowing it was right.

It came out awkward, choppy,

From beneath the word "thirteen."

I shoveled back when people asked,

Because that wasn't right,

Not anymore.

Fourteen had just become familiar.

 Just in time for fifteen.

Fifteen that came too fast

Because fourteen had yet to leave

 And yet to come.

When did thirteen become fourteen?

And when will fourteen become fifteen?

When will I ever feel the age I am?

 And when will I ever be the age I feel?

TRY THIS (as specifically and as quickly as you can for 2–3 minutes)

+ Write out anything this poem brings to mind for you.
+ Borrow any line, letting the line lead your thinking.
+ Think about Annika's questions. Try to answer any one of them for yourself.

© 2018 by Linda Rief from *The Quickwrite Handbook: 100 Mentor Texts to Jumpstart Your Students' Thinking and Writing.* Portsmouth, NH: Heinemann.

TRY THIS (as specifically and as quickly as you can for 2–3 minutes)

✦ Write out anything this excerpt brings to mind for you.

✦ Think of any experience you have had that you would describe as "awesome," because it wasn't necessarily expected (a stranger's fart in an elevator—another anecdote in *The Book of Awesome*—or a snow day, a canceled test, or the smell and sound of a campfire, etc.).

Excerpt from *The Book of Awesome*
by Neil Pasricha

When someone lands on the hotel you just built in Monopoly

Shelling out for that primo real estate on the corner lot ain't always easy.

Yes, you may have to mortgage Electric Company or dip into that stash of hundreds hidden under the game board. But after you make your big investment, there's nothing finer than somebody landing right plum on it, right plum on their next turn.

And there's always a new bit of tension on that first roll after a hotel enters the game too. No more superquick circling and buying properties, collecting Get Out of Jail cards, and winning second place in beauty contests. No, now there's a hotel on the board and you enter Round 2 of Monopoly, where the haves and have-nots are quickly and ruthlessly divided.

When someone lands on the hotel you just built, the first thing they do is get real quiet and quickly pass the dice to the next player, sort of hoping you don't notice that they're squatting on your joint.

But you notice all right.

And maybe you're even all polite and nonchalant about it too.

"Oh, Marvin Gardens? Hold on a second, wait. Yeah, sorry, uh, let's see here. That'll be $1,200, please."

"What, seriously?"

"Yeah, sorry. It's the hotel that does it." (*Passing the property card over for inspection.*)

(*Inspecting property card.*) "That's crazy. That's like all my money. I might have to mortgage Baltic Avenue."

"I'm sorry, man. I'll take all the railroads instead if you want."

(*disgusted*) "What, no way! Then I'll just have Baltic and the blues. Forget it! That's crazy!"

"Fine . . . $1,200, please."

(*angrily and slowly counting out and handing you a thick stack of hundreds, twenties, tens, fives, and ones that barely add up to $1,200, leaving them with only a few properties and two ten-dollar bills*)

AWESOME!

Trichotillomania: More Than Stress
By Isabel S.

You have felt the way that loneliness gnaws and scratches inside your stomach. . .

You have. The night before you sit in your bed crying, not sure what to do. You hear your mother rush in, panting "What's wrong?" You turn around to face her. There is silence for a moment. Your left eyebrow is gone. You slowly open your palm and laying there are the hairs that used to perch upon your face.

Months go by. Now both of your eyebrows are gone and so are your eyelashes.

A year has passed. Now the top of your scalp is bare. You are forced to wear gloves and hats to school. In the summer your gloves are pinned to your clothes. You can't let your hair down anymore or else someone will see the ugly little girl with no hair. Old friends don't want to sit with you anymore because they think you look odd.

You're alone, and you can't stop.

TRY THIS (as specifically and as quickly as you can for 2–3 minutes)

✦ Write out anything that Isabel's writing brings to mind for you.

✦ Borrow any line and write in any direction in which that line leads you.

✦ Write out any feeling that you have experienced that "gnaws and scratches inside your stomach."

✦ Start with a sketch. Show the way you wish you were and the way you often feel, just as Isabel does in her drawing.

TEACHER NOTE Isabel's (not her real name) first line is borrowed from a piece of writing by Michaela Coplen, "Fourteen Months on the Home Front," written when she was sixteen and submitted to The Scholastic Art & Writing Awards in 2012. I read Michaela's piece to my students, asking them to borrow any line that jumped out at them and write as fast as they could from that line. Isabel's piece poured out of her. It left me speechless. I told her how sorry I was and how I wish I knew how to help her. She said just writing it, admitting it, made her feel better and she was working on trying to stop.

TRY THIS (as specifically and as quickly as you can for 2–3 minutes)

+ Write out those things you would rather do instead of the one thing you really dislike doing.

+ Write out anything that comes to mind as you read Adam's cartoons.

I'd Rather . . .
By Adam B.

I'D RATHER SWIM IN SHARK INFESTED WATERS, THAN WRITE.

I'D RATHER BE LOCKED IN A CAGE WITH 47 LIONS, AND A SLAB OF MEAT TIED TO MY BACK, THAN WRITE.

I'D RATHER BE SAT ON BY A SUMO WRESTLER, THAN WRITE.

TEACHER NOTE Have your students look closely at Adam's cartoons and captions. Notice how the things he would "rather do" are far worse than what he claims he dislikes doing. Have your students think about something they really dislike doing. Have them think about those things that in reality would be far worse than what they claim to hate, loathe, or detest doing.

Apparently
By Stacie D.

Apparently, my birth mom didn't hold me
Apparently, she didn't even know who my dad was
She didn't give me a name
Apparently, she never even saw me

My adoptive mom tells me
It is hard to give up a child
It is motherly instinct
Apparently, my birth mom didn't have any
For me

I have pictures
The orphanage workers
Put my hair in a waterfall
The clothes they had for me didn't fit
So they put layers of clothes on me
I looked like a living marshmallow!
Apparently, I was malnourished
When I came to the United States all I knew
Was boiled eggs

Apparently, my birth mom drank when I was inside of her
My adoptive mom says
I have FASD, Fetal Alcohol Spectrum Disorder
I feel like my birth mom didn't care about me
Because
She didn't hold me
She didn't know my dad
She didn't give me a name
She never even saw me

Apparently

TRY THIS (as specifically and as quickly as you can for 2–3 minutes)

✦ Write out anything this poem brings to mind for you.

✦ Borrow any line, letting the line lead your thinking in any direction.

✦ Take the word *apparently*, and write out all that comes to mind when you start with just that word.

Dysphoria
By Seth H.

You think this will solve everything. You get a haircut, believing it'll be enough, you'll finally be happy. But it's not enough. Your life so far is just the prologue, just a dress rehearsal, the story won't start until you're in your body.

One day you look in the mirror. You're making a list of everything terrible about what you see until you realize you're staring at a stranger. You stare at *her* thinking that if you just stare long enough you'll be happy again, you'll find something good in all the chaos, but it's not. You stare until you can't any more, like your brain is a TV but it's been switched to static. The only thing you're able to think is *I want to be normal.* You hear it on repeat until it's all you can think. *I want to be normal.*

You're found sobbing on the cold, tiled bathroom floor, desperately trying to rid yourself of your hips that are too big, your chest that isn't flat, the voice that isn't yours, even your skeleton that is mocking you. You're brought to therapy. You try to talk but you can't find the words to express the agony. You're stuck in a cell that's in the shape of someone else, specially designed to torture you. You're told it will all be all right, and that it will get better with time.

For a while, you believe it. But it hasn't gotten any better yet. It won't come. Now, whenever you hear someone tell you it will get better, you just smile and nod along. You desperately want to believe it. You want to keep hold of the end of the ledge, but you can't hear it anymore.

Every "she," every "ma'am," every "ladies," every "her," you hear directed at you drives you deeper into the static. It's so loud now you can't even hear yourself when you scream. You're shaking relentlessly and you can't remember what it was like before *now*. You don't go outside, you don't shower, you don't get out of bed, you don't go out with friends, you don't escape. Eventually, you'll hope you'll get Stockholm Syndrome, hoping you'll fall in love with your captor. At least then you'll be content.

© 2018 by Linda Rief from *The Quickwrite Handbook: 100 Mentor Texts to Jumpstart Your Students' Thinking and Writing.* Portsmouth, NH: Heinemann.

TEACHER NOTE When we share with our students pieces of writing that are filled with the challenges of another's life, written with clarity and honesty, we have to realize we may get that same clarity and honesty in our students' responses to that writing. They hear the voice of a writer who trusts the reader with his or her story. Our hope is that in the sharing of such poignant writing, our students are developing a deeper and more compassionate understanding of each other.

You can't talk to the people around you because you're afraid that you're just a ghost and they can't see you.

It's been so long now all you're left with is a calendar. Every day is marked with a red X. You count down the days until it will all be okay, and a doctor presents you the key to this cage, counting relentlessly like a child running after the end of a rainbow or a hamster running aimlessly in its wheel. You've been wandering the desert for months, but when you see the oasis in the distance you find that it's just a mirage. All you can do is wait, because your life is the only thing *she* didn't take from you.

TEACHER NOTE Two other especially thoughtful and poignant resources that grapple with gender dysphoria are "Letter to the Girl I Used to Be" by Ethan Smith (YouTube video) and "How to Be a Girl" by Marlo Mack (www.howtobeagirlpodcast.com).

© 2018 by Linda Rief from *The Quickwrite Handbook: 100 Mentor Texts to Jumpstart Your Students' Thinking and Writing.* Portsmouth, NH: Heinemann.

Excerpt from *the first part last*
by Angela Johnson

then

SO HERE'S A GOOD DAY.

We'll call it a fairy tale day.

Once upon a time, really right now, there was this hero (I always wanted to be one) who lived in the city. He was born in the city, loved the city, and never wanted to be anywhere else but the city.

He loved the feel of it. The way you got juiced when you walked down the sidewalk and everybody was out.

He loved the smell of it. Pizza on one corner, falafel and French pastries on the next. Standing in front of the Chinese restaurant, wondering if you want soup or if you just jump a train to that Jamaican place that K-Boy got kicked out of.

He loved the sounds that woke him in the morning and put him to sleep at night. And when he left the city and the noise to go someplace else—another country or town—he missed it.

Couldn't sleep without the ambulance noises and people calling to each other in the street who are just getting back from the clubs.

He couldn't help but get used to the delivery trucks that pulled up early for the restaurants in the neighborhood and the jackhammers and horns. He loved the sounds the kids made running to the subway, and cabs blowing by and screeching to a stop.

Now, 'cause this is a fairy tale, it's important to have some sort of monster, but I've decided not to include him in the story. Decided that because this was a perfect day, we didn't need him along to screw up the magical kingdom and run crazy through the streets, breathing fire and knocking down pizza joints and hot dog stands.

TRY THIS (as specifically and as quickly as you can for 2–3 minutes)

✦ Write out anything this excerpt brings to mind for you.

✦ Start with the line "So here's a ___ day. We'll call it a ___ day." Let the line lead your thinking.

✦ Bobby, the main character in *the first part last,* shows us so clearly what he loves about the city: the sights, the sounds, the smells, the *feel* of the city. Describe what you love about the city, the country, or any other *place* or *event* that gets you "juiced up."

TEACHER NOTE Angela Johnson uses *then* and *now* to move us back and forth through time in this poignant story of an impulsive, restless teenage boy, who learns on his sixteenth birthday that his girlfriend is pregnant. Instead of parties and hanging out with friends he must figure out "the right thing to do."

Using *then* and *now* as a craft technique moves us through time in an engaging way, and metaphorically through all the decisions and emotions with which Bobby is faced. In our students' writing, this may be a way to help them frame a time that propelled them back and forth through a difficult decision.

Leaning Outward

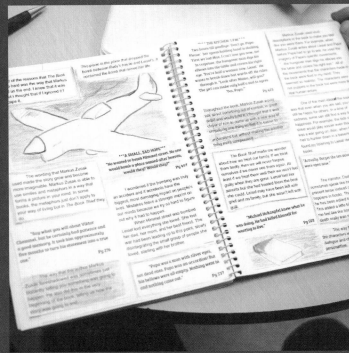

© 2018 by Linda Rief from *The Quickwrite Handbook: 100 Mentor Texts to Jumpstart Your Students' Thinking and Writing.* Portsmouth, NH: Heinemann.

TRY THIS (as specifically and as quickly as you can for 2–3 minutes)

+ Write out all this poem brings to mind for you starting with the line "I am from," listing all the places, the people, the common expressions, the foods, and all the things unique to you.

+ Think of the sights, sounds, smells, touches, and tastes that are all part of your childhood, from your earliest memories to today, and describe as many as you can.

+ Borrow any line, letting the line lead your thinking and writing.

I'm From

By Linda Rief

With thanks to George Ella Lyon after reading her poem "Where I'm From"

I'm from hotdogs, baked beans and brown bread
On Saturday nights—fish sticks on Fridays—pot roast
On Sundays—from Sunday afternoon drives to Howard Johnson's
For clam strips at Nantasket Beach—occasional treats
Of sundaes swimming in hot fudge, whipped cream and walnuts
Brought from Brigham's by my dad

I'm from paper routes, Sunday comics, Camp Aldersgate,
Blood suckers, outdoor showers, bug juice, and gimp bracelets—
Playing softball in the dirt field behind Dunning's, skating
On Hornstra's pond in winter—hot cocoa, snow forts, and
Icicles dangling from woolen mittens

I'm from the top of a ladder picking blueberries
From high bushes, the plinking sound as they fell
Into the coffee can—the playhouse log cabin
In my backyard—the sound of rain washing the roof
As I sat safe, enveloped in the smell of lilacs
A Nancy Drew mystery stretched across my lap

I'm from the Macombers of Scotland and the Gustafsons
Of Sweden—a father who drank vanilla extract when he couldn't find
His scotch or beer—a mother who sat her sadness behind
The Quincy Patriot Ledger and held the car keys
Tightly in her fist

TEACHER NOTE Read George Ella Lyon's poem to your students. It is found in her book *Where I'm From* along with numerous other suggestions for stimulating more writing. Or read my poem to your students along with Ella G.'s piece in the following Interlude. Or just read Ella's piece. Find the one that sparks your students' thinking and share that one with them. You might point out that Ella concentrated on one place, Boston, whereas I wandered around a bit to various locations in my early childhood and adolescence.

Interlude

Ella called her response to George Ella Lyon's poem, written in her writer's-reader's notebook, an "autobiographical snippet" and used it to guide a script for making a video about who she is and where she is from.

I am from . . .
by Ella G.

I am from the street where chain link fences are broken and bent,
And music blares from stereos inside windows and doors,
Houses slouch against each other, tired after long years in the city,
Cigarette butts still smoking on the sidewalk.

I am from the graffiti, the broken glass,
skipping over its shiny shards, in my new white shoes,
tiptoeing on the curb like a tightrope walker,
Arms outstretched, with nowhere to fall.

I am from the house with three floors,
with pipes still echoing with the clangs of Nona's spoon,
calling us to dinner, so many years ago.
Some days, you can almost smell her food cooking.

I am from the smell of new paint, the cottony rollers,
fresh flowers in the kitchen, thick gelato,
dripping down my chin, my spoon forgotten.
Maybe we can watch the Sox play before bedtime.

I am from the old radiator, the bagpipes singing by our house,
Candles burning and car horns honking,
Curled up on the couch with my parents, watching Big Papi hit 'em home.
I am from Boston.

TRY THIS (as quickly and as specifically as you can for 2–3 minutes)

+ List an address where you have some special memories. Borrow Amy Krouse Rosenthal's line "One could count on things. Always: . . ." Think specifically about the sights, sounds, smells, and the ordinary things that you could count on at this address. Who is there? What are they doing? What are the happenings that make it special? What are the things you could count on at this address? *Always.*

+ Write about anything that comes to mind as you read Rosenthal's piece.

Excerpt from *Encyclopedia of an Ordinary Life*
by Amy Krouse Rosenthal

3841 Bordeaux was my address for a very long time. Technically, I lived there eleven years—from the age of three to the age of fourteen—but it felt like a hundred and eleven years. For those were the years when a year was an eternity of days. Time was somewhere between stretched-out and nonexistent. Life wasn't forward-moving then; life just was. It was as big and beautiful and motionless as my mahogany bedroom dresser. 3841 felt as forever to me then as the finiteness of life feels to me now. One could count on things. Always: curled up worms on the sidewalk after it rained. Always: the comforting weekend sound of the Cubs game or the Bears game on TV; the rise and fall of the announcer's voice; the muffled roar of the crowd; not understanding any of it; steady, likable background noise. Always: my dad's bottom drawer of neatly folded white undershirts; being able to take them to sleep in, so soft. Always: holidays with the uncles at the card table playing Hearts. Always: reading the cereal box while we ate breakfast, Beth and I. Always: being in my room, hearing the mechanical chinking of the garage door opening and knowing my parents were home. Always: my dad whistling and dressed nicely, even on Sundays, a sweater and pressed slacks. Always: my mom shaving in the tub, one leg hovering in the air, razor gracefully raking from ankle up to knee. Always: getting into bed and feeling the cold underside of the pillow against my forearm. Always: the late-night lullaby of ice knocking against my parents' water glasses as they came upstairs. There were a lot of always's. Even today the number 3841 sounds more like infinity to me than the word *infinity* itself.

TEACHER NOTE You might help your students notice that Rosenthal uses the word *Always* to shift to a new topic. If she stays on the topic she uses only a semi-colon to separate specifics about that topic.

My Hand
by Linda Rief

Trace the outline of your hand onto a blank page in your writer's-reader's notebook or onto any blank piece of paper, just as I have done here. Leave it blank for the moment while your teacher shows a video of Sarah Kay speaking aloud her poem "Hands."

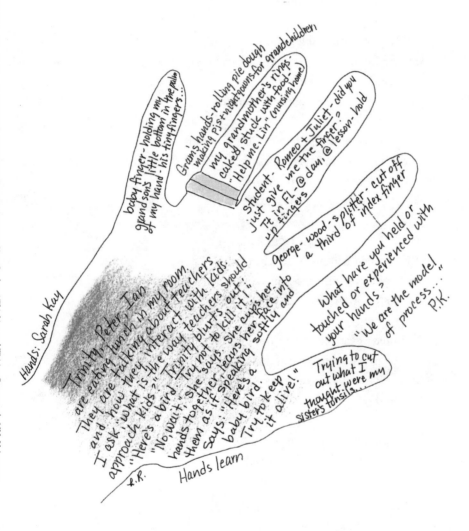

TRY THIS (as specifically and as quickly as you can for 2–3 minutes)

+ Underneath, or around, the outline of your hand, jot down any phrases from Sarah Kay's poem that jump out at you and/or remind you of something in your own life or the world around you.

+ Borrow one of those lines or phrases and write down all that comes to mind, letting the line lead your thinking and writing.

+ When you have more time, on each finger in the sketch of your hand, jot down phrases that will get you back to a story connected to your hand or that particular finger—"a story that shows something that you have held or touched or experienced with that hand or finger." (Penny Kittle)

TEACHER NOTE Draw your own hand, as your students draw theirs. Sarah Kay's spoken word poem "Hands" can be found on YouTube. You can have students simply listen and jot phrases she uses that bring something to mind for them, or give them a copy of the text of the poem after they listen to her, to reread and underline the phrases significant to them, from which to write. When you and your students have more time, fill in your own sketch of your hand with words or phrases connected to your stories, as your students are filling in theirs.

© 2018 by Linda Rief from *The Quickwrite Handbook: 100 Mentor Texts to Jumpstart Your Students' Thinking and Writing.* Portsmouth, NH: Heinemann.

TRY THIS (as quickly and as specifically as you can for 2–3 minutes)

+ Write out anything this poem brings to mind.

+ Borrow any line, letting the line lead your thinking.

The Last Time I Bumped into Don Murray
by Ralph Fletcher

The last time I bumped into Don Murray
his 83-year-old hands were long,
white, blue-veined, tremulous
but strong when we shook hands.

Those hands carried a gun in war,
and broke up fights between soldiers.
At fifty they signed the legal paper
to take his daughter off life support.

I'd watch him offer a hand to his frail wife,
not to lift her up, as he explained it,
but as a fixed point in the world
she could pull against to stand.

The hands gestured as he talked:
"Even when Minnie Mae was dying
I was able to finish most projects—
I did a lot of writing in my head."

I pointed at his hand: "You're bleeding."
The waitress fetched a Bandaid.
his hands such a river of trembling
he could not manage to unwrap it.

So he finally let me do it for him,
more amused than embarrassed,
muttering about new medication,
as I tenderly covered the small wound.

TEACHER NOTE Use this piece by Ralph Fletcher and/or the next piece by Jessica Ryan as additional mentor pieces about hands, helping students see how different they are. You might show them all three and then have them draw their hand or spread the three pieces and the drawing out over three or four days to give them time to think about ideas.

My Father's Habit
by Jessica Ryan

My father overuses his middle finger. He uses it to point with authority—things should be done this way and not that. He uses it to give directions—"Go down Banfield Road, take a right, follow the road and you'll end up at the beach."

But he never, ever uses it to tell someone how and where to shove something. He never uses it to show hatred, to accuse, to condemn. A street youth from Somerville, you would think he would know how to use the middle finger correctly.

As a child, I tried to change this habit. Constantly complaining, with the knowledgeable arrogance of an eight-year-old, I would tell him "The middle finger was not meant to do what the pointer finger does." I think he used it purposefully, always hoping to see my eyes roll toward heaven, praying and thinking, "Oh, dear Lord, no. Here we go again." But he would just look at me with eyes blue enough to glow and laugh, always amused that I could get so worked up about a small thing like using the wrong finger.

As an adult, if someone showed me a picture of 100 hands with the middle finger up, my father's would jump out at me, screaming into the deep recesses of memory: "Jesska, it's me!" I would recognize his hands, tough and marked from years of hard work and war. His hands held guns. The ones fired in battles in foreign lands and dense jungles where young men died. Knowing now that the pointer finger is the one to squeeze triggers, I wonder if that is why he never uses it. Others once viewed his hands as dangerous, his fingers as ticking time bombs.

But from his hands I have only known support when I have faltered. When I've lost direction and felt like a boat lost on an unforgiving sea, floating without a sure destination, he would subtly lift his middle finger and give a point. When seeking absolution for an endless list of completely avoidable mistakes and wrongdoings, he would use his middle finger to point to his own chest to show that he, too, has made mistakes— and forgiveness would always be given.

TRY THIS (as quickly and as specifically as you can for 2–3 minutes)

+ Write out anything this poem brings to mind.
+ Borrow any line, letting the line lead your thinking.

© 2018 by Linda Rief from *The Quickwrite Handbook: 100 Mentor Texts to Jumpstart Your Students' Thinking and Writing*. Portsmouth, NH: Heinemann.

TRY THIS (as quickly and as specifically as you can for 2–3 minutes)

✦ In writing capture all Abigail's poem brings to mind for you.

✦ Borrow any line, such as "If I had a life I could live," "The night holds on to me tightly," "I'd travel to places unknown," or any other line that resonates with you. Let the line lead your thinking.

✦ Who do you carry around in your heart? Describe all you can about that relationship.

Edge of Life
by Abigail Lynne Becker

If I had a life I could live
Then I'd travel to places unknown.
With you in my heart, I'd begin at the start
And never would I be alone.

A voice in the evening is calling
It tears at my soul like a fire.
Yet I cannot forget the time when we met
And the burning of that newfound desire.

I love you, I say in the darkness
I feel that I must hold you near.
Yet you slip through my grasp, like the hours gone past
And that voice is still all I can hear.

It tells me to travel to mountains
And to places where valleys are green.
Yet it's hard to let go of the things that I know
And the love and the hardship I've seen.

If I had a dream I could give you
I would wrap it in velvet and pearls
And send it away on the rush of the wind
That would carry it over the world.

TEACHER NOTE Your students might like to know something about Abigail. She died at the age of sixteen in an automobile accident caused by a driver making an illegal U-turn. Jim Christensen, a family friend, said of Abi: "She knew friendship and she knew loneliness. She knew joy and she knew sadness. She knew peace and she knew turmoil. She didn't shrink from life. She lived life." Abi's parents and sisters collected her writing and drawings into a collection they titled *A Box of Rain*. "Edge of Life" is a song Abi wrote for guitar accompaniment.

The night holds on to me tightly
And she won't let me out in the cold.
I've reaped what I've sown, and I've called this place home
Still I'm searching for something to hold.

If I had a life I could live
Then I'd travel to places unknown.
With you in my heart, I'd begin at the start
And never would I be alone.

With tears in my eyes I speak to you
Through the blindness of good and of bad
Please forget what I've said, for the feelings are dead.
You're the best friend that I've ever had.

And if I had a dream I could give you
I'd wrap you in velvet and pearls
And send it away on the rush of the wind
That would carry it over the world.
I still have a life I'm not living.
I must get to those places unknown.
With you in my heart, I will end where I start
And never will I be alone.

© 2018 by Linda Rief from *The Quickwrite Handbook: 100 Mentor Texts to Jumpstart Your Students' Thinking and Writing*. Portsmouth, NH: Heinemann.

TRY THIS (as quickly and as specifically as you can for 2–3 minutes)

✦ Borrow any line, and write from that line, letting the line lead your thinking.

✦ Describe anything this anecdote brings to mind for you, leaving the description in the third person *he* or *she*, or changing the pronoun to first-person *I* or second-person *you*.

✦ Try describing an experience you've had by using time, as Skolnick does, to create and build on the tension. Let the reader know what you are thinking or feeling as the tension builds.

✦ Use present tense instead of past tense to create a feeling of being in the moment.

Excerpt from *One Breath*
by Adam Skolnick

He looked calm, but appearances can be deceiving . . . it was the only competition that mattered to him and most others in the sport, and Nick was out of juice. Every muscle in his body hurt. Even his lungs hurt, but he wasn't about to give up. It was game day, . . .

"Four minutes!"

He inhaled long and slow and exhaled twice as slow, twice as calm. Each time purging his system of negativity and carbon dioxide, the buildup of which spurs that urge to breathe and can turn a relaxed, peaceful adventure into excruciating toil. . . . That was the only way to lower his heart rate, and keep his demons at bay.

"Three minutes!"

He knew them well, his demons. They'd trailed him his entire life. They fueled him. His broken home, his feelings of inadequacy, his frustration with society attuned to greed and waste, were what drove him into the water in the first place . . . he had one more dive in him, . . .

"Two minutes!"

TEACHER NOTE You might use this piece to point out a craft move—the use of time to build tension and anxiety, not only in Nick but also in the reader.

Penny
by Kerri B.

Her little eyes peer,

Waiting for my glance.

Tail wiggles,

Ears perk.

Sad eyes stare me down.

Guilt sinks in,

And I become a slave

To throw and fetch.

I throw, she fetches.

I throw, she fetches.

I try to escape to the house,

But those eyes drag me back.

Those adorable, irresistible eyes.

Yes, her little tipped ears

And her incessantly wagging tail

Can make a person's conscience act.

But her eyes can imprison you

In a never-ending game

Of throw and fetch

Throw and fetch.

TRY THIS (as quickly and as specifically as you can for 2–3 minutes)

+ Borrow any line to begin your writing, letting the line guide your thinking.
+ Write out anything that Kerri's words bring to mind for you.
+ Write out all the ways an animal or pet captures your attention.

© 2018 by Linda Rief from *The Quickwrite Handbook: 100 Mentor Texts to Jumpstart Your Students' Thinking and Writing.* Portsmouth, NH: Heinemann.

Rosemarie Stewart

by Mel Glenn

TRY THIS (as quickly and as
specifically as you can for 2–3
minutes)

✦ Write out anything this poem
brings to mind for you.

✦ Borrow any word or line, and
write all that the word or line
brings to mind, letting the line
lead your thinking.

✦ In what ways has the "starring
role" of a sibling or classmate
been a frustration for you?

Responsible,

Trustworthy,

Kind,

Quiet,

Obedient,

A girl scout without the uniform.

You would think all that is enough to win

My parents' love.

But in the theater of our house

Brenda holds center stage. She is

Irresponsible,

Sneaky,

Mean,

Loud,

Rebellious.

Her negative traits far outweigh the 100s I bring home.

When the cops called I felt sad,

Not for the trouble she was in,

But for the fact that once again

She cast herself in the starring role.

Poem for an Inked Daughter
by Jean Wyrick

I did it too you know, just differently.
Way back then
when I was angry, young
I pierced my ears with a rusty ice pick,
and willfully wore dangly earrings
(and a smirk) to Christmas dinner.
My scandalized mother
referred to me for days as
"my daughter, the dirty gypsy."
I let my ears jingle silver music, ultimately
dancing right over her Victorian disapproval
out of that house forever.

And now here you are,
fresh from a different kind of parlor,
with that defiant dragon
curling dark over your shoulder.
No, of course you know I don't like it.
Another gauntlet thrown down
in the ongoing Mother-Daughter Wars.

But hear this, my own gypsy girl:
I know something you don't.
That under that fierce fire-breathing dragon,
claws bared, ready for the next battle,
under the skin where the purple ink turns to blood,
your blood is my blood,
rushing red to red, flowing in a long bond
linking my heart to you no matter what,
like the swirling, twisting lines
of an intricate intimate tattoo,
invisible, indelible, forever permanent.

TRY THIS (as quickly and as specifically as you can, for 2–3 minutes)

+ Write out anything this poem brings to mind for you.

+ Borrow any line from the poem, letting the line lead your thinking as you write.

+ In what ways does this poem remind you of yourself or someone you know?

+ Thinking about Wyrick's line "another gauntlet thrown down in the ongoing Mother-Daughter Wars," what does this line bring to mind for you?

TEACHER NOTE "The Tattoo Dragon," a poem by Kathi Appelt, might be a good poem to link with this one. Either one, or both of them together, might lead to a rich discussion of those things we all do, or did, to individualize ourselves.

© 2018 by Linda Rief from *The Quickwrite Handbook: 100 Mentor Texts to Jumpstart Your Students' Thinking and Writing.* Portsmouth, NH: Heinemann.

TRY THIS (as quickly and as specifically as you can for 2–3 minutes)

+ Write out anything that this excerpt brings to mind for you.

+ Too many people are given a hard time about their body image, yet no one is perfect. Write out anything this excerpt brings to mind about body image, either something that may have been said to you or to someone you know, or that you have overheard said to someone else.

+ Borrow any line or phrase, letting the line lead your thinking.

Excerpt from *Butter*
by Erin Jade Lange

You think I eat a lot now? That's nothing. Tune in December 31st, when I will stream a live webcast of my last meal. Death row inmates get one. Why shouldn't I? I can't take another year in this fat suit, but I can end this year with a bang. If you can stomach it, you're invited to watch . . . as I eat myself to death.

Most people would say the website is where this wild ride began. But it started two days earlier . . . with this story on the news about airlines charging obese people for two airplane seats.

Look, I get it. It sucks to be next to the fat guy on the plane. Maybe he's taking up too much of your armrest or crowding you into the window, but trust me, nobody's more uncomfortable than that guy, having to squish into that tiny seat and knowing nobody wants to sit next to him. The humiliation is payment enough, let alone an extra charge. . . .

I was getting riled up watching the story, when I looked down and remembered two airline seats were the least of my worries. Right then, I was taking up two cushions on the couch. My eyes slid from the cushions to the coffee table. An empty candy dish with crumbles of peanut M&Ms, a half-melted tub of ice cream, and a bag of Doritos were just a few of the spoils before me. A single Dorito was balanced precariously on the edge of the bag. I rescued it before it fell and transferred it to my mouth.

On Visiting My Great-Aunt Who Lived in a Three-Decker in Dorchester

by Linda Rief

I hated Aunt Judy's polyester dresses, thick stockings, crooked seams, square-heeled shoes, tightly frizzed permed hair, coke-bottle glasses, and wet smooches that slid down my cheek. So I turned her cream to butter, flushed her chain toilet over and over again, and climbed onto her brocade sofa with dirty shoes, while she yelled, "No, no, Linda! Stop the beater. No, no, Linda! Don't flush that again! No, no, Linda, not on Great-Grammy's sofa!" So I pushed off hard with my foot and climbed onto the stool of the player piano, locked my fingers underneath the keys, slid to the edge until my toes reached the pedals and pumped hard until the paper songs flapped and slapped endlessly on the roll.

Sent outside "to play" I pulled all the strawberry plants from her backyard garden and handed her the nosegay of white petals hoping she'd yell at me, but she took them in hand like an old maid bride with a thank you and a warm smile for my father so that I couldn't back away from her musty, mothball smell that choked my air or the rhinestone broach that pricked my skin when she pulled me in close and pinched my arms together so tight that I folded like an accordion and whispered, so close that my face was showered with her spit, and so close that my father couldn't hear, "Be good, for goodness sake, or I'll slap your *behind* when your father isn't looking!"

TRY THIS (as specifically and as quickly as you can for 2–3 minutes)

✦ Write out anything this character sketch brings to mind for you.

✦ Borrow any line, letting the line lead your thinking.

✦ I don't know why I was so mean to my great-aunt. I think it might have been because she liked my sister more than she did me. (I can understand why!) Think of someone to whom you have been mean, who has been mean to you, or to whom others have been mean, and write out how you or others treated this person.

✦ Think about someone to whom you have been *kind*, or who has been *kind* to you. Describe all the ways you, or they, have shown that kindness.

✦ Change any of the writing you did to first-person *I*, second-person *you*, or third-person *he* or *she*, and notice how it changes the writing.

© 2018 by Linda Rief from *The Quickwrite Handbook: 100 Mentor Texts to Jumpstart Your Students' Thinking and Writing*. Portsmouth, NH: Heinemann.

TRY THIS (as specifically and as quickly as you can for 2–3 minutes)

+ Write out anything this excerpt brings to mind for you.

+ Think about a unique character that you know well or might not know well. Describe what you do know about this person.

+ Think about someone you know well and describe what you know they have never done or seen or said and what you know they have done that they are good at.

+ Describe yourself in the same way Capote lets us see this woman. Describe what you have never done that might surprise others. Describe some specific things you are good at and have done.

Excerpt from *A Christmas Memory*
By Truman Capote

A woman with shorn white hair is standing at the kitchen window. She is wearing tennis shoes and a shapeless gray sweater over a summery calico dress. She is small and sprightly, like a bantam hen; but, due to a long youthful illness, her shoulders are pitifully hunched. Her face is remarkable—not unlike Lincoln's, craggy like that, and tinted by sun and wind; but it is delicate too, finely boned, and her eyes are sherry-colored and timid.

. . . In addition to never having seen a movie, she has never: eaten in a restaurant, traveled more than five miles from home, received or sent a telegram, read anything except funny papers and the Bible, worn cosmetics, cursed, wished someone harm, told a lie on purpose, let a hungry dog go hungry. Here are a few things she has done, does do: killed with a hoe the biggest rattlesnake ever seen in this county (sixteen rattles), dip snuff (secretly), tame hummingbirds (just try it) till they balanced on her finger, tell ghost stories (we both believe in ghosts) so tingling they chill you in July, talk to herself, take walks in the rain, grow the prettiest japonicas in town, know the recipe for every sort of old-time Indian cure, including a magical wart-remover.

TEACHER NOTE You might remind your students that writing often starts with a memorable person or character. In their writing, this character description or description of self might lead to a memoir piece because that person is central to that memory. Or their description might just sit in their notebook until they recognize the way it fits into a bigger, more substantial piece.

Walking Down a Stone Driveway
by Dana S.

Piles of gold line the loose stones,

Curled at the edges,

Huddling together for warmth in the cold, crisp fall air.

The drive looks like a tunnel of gold

Sweeping together at the top

With pieces of brilliant blue tracing through the branches.

The moss slowly crawls down the stone floor,

Slowly unrolling a carpet

For the final clash of colors,

Before the ancient ceilings crumble into brown piles.

And people drive by

So fast.

TRY THIS (as specifically and as quickly as you can for 2–3 minutes)

+ Write out anything Dana's poem brings to mind for you.

+ Borrow any line and let the line lead your thinking.

+ Think of a single sight that either pleases or bothers you and describe that sight as completely as you can.

+ Dana describes the wealth of beauty that exists in this one scene that we so often take for granted and seldom notice. What is something you pass by every day that you haven't really looked at? When you really look, what do you see?

© 2018 by Linda Rief from *The Quickwrite Handbook: 100 Mentor Texts to Jumpstart Your Students' Thinking and Writing.* Portsmouth, NH: Heinemann.

TRY THIS (as specifically and as quickly as you can for 2–3 minutes)

✦ Write out anything that this poem brings to mind for you.

✦ Borrow one of the lines, letting the line lead your thinking.

✦ What is "adolescence" like for you? What makes this time in your life "confusing" or "dangerous" or always taking "unexpected turns"?

A Slice of Life
by Katherine T.

What's as confusing as last week's science lab?

Can be as sweet as sugar?

Then, sharp as a knife?

Comes quickly

But with no instructions on how to handle it?

Can take you up to the stars

Or throw you sprawling against a rock?

Just when you think you've got it figured out

It takes an unexpected turn

Those who have lived it

Either warn you about the dangers it brings

Or tell you to live it to the fullest

Perhaps you know what I am talking about

Don't let it pass by without making a mark

Or saving a memory, because

It will only come once, and soon the opportunities

The moments, the dreams

Will all just be a slice of your past

The pieces of life that we call

Adolescence

Excerpt from *Miss Peregrine's Home for Peculiar Children*
by Ransom Riggs

I had just come to accept that my life would be ordinary when extraordinary things began to happen. The first of these came as a terrible shock and, like anything that changes you forever, split my life into halves: Before and After.

Excerpt from *A Northern Light*
by Jennifer Donnelly

Right now I want a word that describes the feeling you get—a cold, sick feeling deep down inside—when you know something is happening that will change you, and you don't want it to, but you can't stop it. And you know, for the very first time, that there will be a *before* and an *after*, a *was* and a *will be*. And that you will never again be quite the same person you were. I imagine it's the feeling Eve had as she bit into the apple. Or Hamlet when he saw his father's ghost. Or Jesus as a boy, right after someone sat him down and told him his father wasn't a carpenter after all.

TRY THIS (as specifically and as quickly as you can for 2–3 minutes)

✦ Write out anything that comes to mind after reading these excerpts.

✦ What event in your life—either personal or in the world at large—has split you into halves: a *Before* and an *After*? What was life like *before*, and how has it changed *after*?

✦ What event in the world has had a profound effect on a number of people and can be seen as a marker of how life was *before*, and how it has changed *after*. Describe not only the event but also what life was like *before* and what it is like now in the *after*.

TRY THIS (as specifically and as quickly as you can for 2–3 minutes)

+ Write out anything this excerpt brings to mind for you.

+ Borrow any line, letting the line lead your thinking.

+ Sometimes, unfortunately, we are "putty in the wrong hands" and get ourselves in trouble. In what ways has that ever happened to you?

Excerpt from *The Follower*
by Jack Gantos

My mother said he was trouble the first time I met him. His name was Frankie Pagoda and he had just catapulted across his yard like a human cannonball and landed badly in ours. He was moaning as I stood over him, not knowing what to do. He was on his back and at first he wasn't moving, but slowly he began to gyrate his arms and legs like a stunned crab.

"Who are you?" I asked.

"Frankie . . . P___" he slowly replied. "Frankie Pagoda."

He was in a lot of pain, and here's what was going on. His older brother, Scary Gary, who had already been in trouble with the law, had made him climb to the very top of a reedy Australian pine tree with a rope between his teeth. Then he tied the rope to the top of the tree and Gary tied the other end to the winch on Mr. Pagoda's tow truck. He winched the tip of the tree all the way down so it made a big spring and then Frankie held on like a koala bear while Gary cut the rope with a machete. Frankie was launched like the stones the Romans flung at the Vandals.

". . . If I ever catch you playing with that kid . . . , you will be in big trouble, . . ." she said.

"You are a follower, not a leader," she said bluntly. "You are putty in the wrong hands. . . ."

I knew this was true but I didn't want to admit it to her.

But within a week I was Frankie's man, which was pretty scary because he was Gary's man, which made me low man on the totem pole—or pine tree.

Excerpt from *The Sun Is Also a Star*
by Nicola Yoon

In fifteenth-century African civilizations, hairstyles were markers of identity. Hairstyle could indicate everything from tribe or family background to religion to social status. Elaborate hairstyles designated power and wealth. A subdued style could be a sign that you were in a state of mourning. More than that, hair could have spiritual importance. Because it's on your head—the highest part of your body and closest to the skies—many Africans viewed it as a passageway for spirits to the soul, a way to interact with God.

That history was erased with the dawn of slavery. On slave ships, newly captured Africans were forcibly shaved in a profound act of dehumanization, an act that effectively severed the link between hair and cultural identity. . . .

Since post-slavery days and through to modern times, debate has raged in the African American community. What does it mean to wear your hair natural versus straightened? Is straightening your hair a form of self-hatred? Does it mean you think your hair in its natural state is not beautiful? If you wear your hair naturally, are you making a political statement, claiming black power? . . .

When Natasha decides to wear hers in an Afro, it's not because she's aware of all of this history. She does it despite Patricia Kingsley's assertions that Afros make women more militant and unprofessional. Those assertions are rooted in fear—fear that her daughter will be harmed by a society that still so often fears blackness. Patricia also doesn't raise her other objection: Natasha's new hairstyle feels like a rejection. She's been relaxing her own hair all her life. She'd relaxed Natasha's since she was ten years old. These days when Patricia looks at her daughter, she doesn't see as much reflected back as before, and it hurts. But of course, all teenagers do this. All teenagers separate from their parents. To grow up is to grow apart.

TRY THIS (as specifically and as quickly as you can for 2–3 minutes)

+ Write out anything this excerpt brings to mind for you.
+ Borrow any line, letting the line lead your thinking.
+ In what ways is your hair important to you?
+ In what ways has your hair caused a commotion or disagreement with parents or anyone else you know?

TEACHER NOTE You might couple this excerpt with "Hairs" from *The House on Mango Street* by Sandra Cisneros, or an excerpt about hair in Chapter 5 of *The Outsiders* by S. E. Hinton, or information about what the Nazis did with all the hair they shaved from prisoners in the concentration camps during World War II.

© 2018 by Linda Rief from *The Quickwrite Handbook: 100 Mentor Texts to Jumpstart Your Students' Thinking and Writing.* Portsmouth, NH: Heinemann.

TRY THIS (as quickly and as specifically as you can for 2–3 minutes)

✦ Write out anything Alison's piece brings to mind for you.

✦ Borrow any line, letting the line lead your thinking.

✦ Change any of the pronouns to the second-person *you*, and let this new line in the second person lead your thinking.

✦ Borrow Alison's title "She Thinks I Don't Know" and let that line lead your thinking. Change the pronouns to any other pronouns as you write.

She Thinks I Don't Know
by Alison A.

I hug my knees to my chest and press my back against the cold metal of my bed. I hear the squeak of her door closing, her feet heavy on the floor. I hear the faint thumps of things being moved, and suddenly, the clink of a bottle to glass pierces the room, too shrill and high for my ears. Too painful for me. Mom's drinking. Again.

She thinks she's so clever, the way she hides it under things in her room. But I find it. She thinks she's so good, the way she covers her breath with cinnamon candies and mints. But I smell it—the hot, putrid stink of wine that makes me want to cry, to puke, to faint, to yell all at the same time. I hate that smell.

What is going through her mind as she savors her forbidden drink? Does she think of the pain it brings to David, and Dad, and me to see her like this? Does she think of how embarrassed I am to have friends over, especially when it's really bad?

She thinks I don't know. I wish I didn't.

Kirsten J.

She Thinks I Don't Know
by Danielle W.

She thinks I don't see that she's

"just a bit thinner" than normal

But I do, yes, I do

From the moment I saw her I knew things were not right because

This was not the same girl I saw last summer or the summer before

The one who loved food, now the one who won't touch it

Who only eats salad and mustard and Splenda

The words scream out to her

Fat free Fat free

So strong, yet now she fades away

She thinks I don't realize she doesn't eat a thing

She thinks I don't see the goose-bumps on her arm

Shivering, the bones showing through

Her skin calling out

Save me

Her frail expression

Her heart. . . slowly

Draining

Away

She thinks I don't know

But I do

Yes

I

Do

TEACHER NOTE Writing leads to more writing, even of different genres. Danielle took Alison's title and wrote several pages, beginning as a quickwrite and developing into the poem. She also realized she wanted to know much more about anorexia nervosa and researched the topic at length for informational writing about a health issue. Notice how Danielle shaped this poem: how even the number of words on a line emphasize what is happening to her cousin. Our words matter, but how we choose to lay them out on the page matters also.

© 2018 by Linda Rief from *The Quickwrite Handbook: 100 Mentor Texts to Jumpstart Your Students' Thinking and Writing.* Portsmouth, NH: Heinemann.

TRY THIS (as specifically and as quickly as you can for 2–3 minutes)

+ Write out anything this excerpt brings to mind for you.

+ Borrow any word, phrase, or line, letting the line lead your thinking.

+ Using Hopkins' frame for the writing, start with *How*, *Why*, *Where*, *When*, *Who*, or *What*, and see if you can connect them all the way she did.

+ Think about an abstract word (*happiness*, *sadness*, *anger*, *jealousy*, *procrastination*, etc.) and try Hopkins' style (or any style) in writing your thinking about that word.

Excerpt from *Perfect*
by Ellen Hopkins

How

    do you define a word without concrete meaning? To each his own, the saying goes, so

Why

    push to attain an ideal state of being that no two random people will agree is

Where

    you want to be? Faultless. Finished. Incomparable. People can never be these, and anyway,

When

    did creating a flawless façade become a more vital goal than learning to love the person

Who

    lives inside your skin? The outside belongs to others; only you should decide for you—

What

    is perfect.

After reading the excerpt from *Perfect* by Ellen Hopkins, Maegan D. wrote the following in her writer's-reader's notebook:

This excerpt helped me realize that perfection doesn't mean anything. It's not the same to everyone. Some people may think it means pretty, thin, and popular. Some people may think it means thoughtful, caring, and kind. But really, perfection doesn't define you. This poem made me think that there is no reason in trying to be something that no one really knows what that something means. Being "perfect" has always been a goal for a lot of girls, but it's hard to achieve something that is not possible. Nothing is ever perfect or flawless. This poem really flicked a switch for me. I feel crazy for ever thinking I needed to be perfect.

TEACHER NOTE Maegan's words stayed as they were written in her notebook. She never developed them into a more extensive piece. They are there *if* and *when* she can use them. It might be helpful for students to see that all writing does not lead to a best draft.

© 2018 by Linda Rief from *The Quickwrite Handbook: 100 Mentor Texts to Jumpstart Your Students' Thinking and Writing.* Portsmouth, NH: Heinemann.

TRY THIS (as specifically and as quickly as you can for 2–3 minutes)

✦ Write out anything this excerpt brings to mind for you.

✦ Borrow any line, letting the line lead your thinking.

✦ What are you like, who are you, on the outside? What are you like, who are you, on the inside?

Excerpt from *Catalyst*
by Laurie Halse Anderson

I like to run at night. No one watches me. No one hears my sneakers slipping in the loose gravel at the side of the road. Gravity doesn't exist. My muscles don't hurt. I float, drift past churches, stores, and schools, past the locked houses and the flicker-blue windows. My mind is quiet and clear. . . .

On the outside I am Good Kate, Rev. Jack Malone's girl, isn't she sweet, she helps so much with the house, so sad about her mother, and she's smart, too, seen her name in the papers for honor roll this and science fair that, she's got scholarship written all over her, runs pretty fast, she's so good with her brother, why can't all teenagers be like her?

A ghost hovers over my left shoulder. I can almost hear her breathe. . . .

On the inside I am Bad Kate, daughter of no one, she's such a bitch, thinks she's all that, prays with her eyes open, lets her boyfriend put his hands all over her, Miss Perfect, Miss Suck-up, disrespectful, disagreeable, still waters run deep and dirty, she's going to lose it, just you watch, I've seen her type before.

Run faster.

Sweat trickles along the bones of my face and licks my neck. Running, sweating, evaporating . . . I'm distilling myself in the dark: mixture, substance, compound, element, atom. The ghost is getting closer. Run faster. Push beyond the wall, push beyond my limits. . . .

The first night I ran like this, the puddles were filmed with ice. Now the trees are leafing and the roads are dry and I fly almost naked, breathless, running out of the empty night into a place where I can hear myself think.

I wish I never had to stop.

Excerpt from *Waiting for You*
by Susane Colasanti

The thing about having an anxiety disorder is that you never quite fit in with everyone else. Not like that's a bad thing. But when all you want to do is function like a normal human being, not fitting in makes your problems a million times bigger. Last year, I was antisocial and depressed and always thinking these negative things. Life kept moving all around me, but I wasn't really involved in any of it. I watched everyone else doing all the things I thought I was supposed to be doing. Those things looked so easy for them, like joining clubs and doing the school play. But I always felt like such an act if I tried to fit in the way normal kids did.

TRY THIS (as specifically and as quickly as you can for 2–3 minutes)

+ Write out anything this excerpt brings to mind for you.

+ Borrow any line, such as, "The thing about having," or "not fitting in," or "I watched everyone else." Let the line lead your thinking.

+ In what ways is fitting in a good thing or a bad thing?

+ In what ways do you prefer to fit in or not fit in?

TRY THIS (as specifically and as quickly as you can for 2–3 minutes)

- Write anything that one or both of these two poems brings to mind for you.

- Borrow any line, letting the line lead your thinking.

- Think about a place with which you are especially familiar: city block, corner grocery, coffee shop, roof of an apartment building, open market, concert, hockey rink, bowling alley, tree stand for hunting, a particular bus stop where you wait, the place you live or the place you visit, and so on. Write out the sights, sounds, smells, and feelings that describe that place well.

Where I Live
by Wesley McNair

You will come into an antique town
whose houses move apart
as if you've interrupted
a private discussion. This is the place
you must pass through to get there.
Imagining lives tucked in
like china plates, continue driving.
Beyond the landscaped streets,
beyond the last colonial gas station
and unsolved by zoning,
is a road. It will take you
to old farmhouses and trees
with car-tire swings.
Signs will announce hairdressing
and night crawlers.
The timothy grass will run beside you
all the way to where I live.

© 2018 by Linda Rief from *The Quickwrite Handbook: 100 Mentor Texts to Jumpstart Your Students' Thinking and Writing*. Portsmouth, NH: Heinemann.

TEACHER NOTE Show both "Where I live" and "City Life" by Sheryl Nelms (on the following page) together to your students, and then ask them to Try This as noted above.

City Life
by Sheryl L. Nelms

at dawn
when Mercury
still hangs
in the west
and the scattered
night clouds
are beginning
to turn pink
around the edges

and the streetlights
down across the valley
sparkle
bright
through the rising
river mist

and a row
of crows
lifts off
out of the cottonwoods
along the river
to become black
silhouettes
over the new sun

city life doesn't seem so bad

Interlude

In his writer's-reader's notebook, Neville wrote in response to Wesley McNair's poem "Where I Live":

Where I Live
by Neville C.

Notice the colors as you drive to my house, like an old oil painting in a vintage frame. The trees become a blur, like an old motion picture, only interrupted by the dark static of a building.

The colors will change. There will be reds, yellows, blues hemmed into the edges of dainty antique houses and tulip petals. The traffic will slow. Cars become sparse. Then you will come upon my house, an old yellow cape with spruce green shutters and daffodils glowing with sunshine.

© 2018 by Linda Rief from *The Quickwrite Handbook: 100 Mentor Texts to Jumpstart Your Students' Thinking and Writing*. Portsmouth, NH: Heinemann.

Notice the drawing Neville did in response to his words. Try your hand at drawing what you wrote—or at least a segment of it.

TEACHER NOTE You might show your students Neville's notebook entry along with his drawing after they've done their quickwrite. Neville did this drawing on his own in his writer's-reader's notebook after responding to the McNair poem. He loves drawing. Offer this as an option to your students. So many of them can *show* us their thinking through drawing.

Excerpt from *The Crossover*
by Kwame Alexander

"Mom, since you asked, I'll tell you why I'm so angry"

Because Dad tried to dunk.

Because I want to win a championship.

Because I can't win a championship if I'm sitting in this smelly hospital.

Because Dad told you he'd be here forever.

Because I thought forever was like Mars—far away.

Because it turns out forever is like the mall—right around the corner.

Because Jordan doesn't talk basketball anymore.

Because Jordan cut my hair and didn't care.

Because he's always drinking Sweet Tea.

Because sometimes I get thirsty.

Because I don't have anybody to talk to now.

Because CPR DOESN'T WORK!

Because my crossover should be better.

Because if it was better, then Dad wouldn't have had the ball.

Because if Dad hadn't had the ball, then he wouldn't have tried to dunk.

Because if Dad hadn't tried to dunk, then we wouldn't be here.

Because I don't want to be *here.*

Because the only thing that matters is *swish.*

Because our backboard is splintered.

TRY THIS (as specifically and as quickly as you can for 2–3 minutes)

+ Write out anything this excerpt brings to mind for you.

+ Borrow any line and let the line lead your thinking as you write.

+ Using Kwame's title, change it to any other person: _____, since you asked, I'll tell you why I'm so _____.

+ Once you begin, try listing every reason with "because," or any other word that makes sense in your writing.

© 2018 by Linda Rief from *The Quickwrite Handbook: 100 Mentor Texts to Jumpstart Your Students' Thinking and Writing*. Portsmouth, NH: Heinemann.

Excerpt from *The Sky Is Everywhere*
by Jandy Nelson

In this book Lennie has already been abandoned by her mother, and now she must cope with the death of her sister, Bailey.

Grief is a house
where the chairs
have forgotten how to hold us
the mirrors how to reflect us
Grief is a house that disappears
each time someone knocks at the door
or rings the bell
a house that blows into the air
at the slightest gust
that buries itself deep in the ground
while everyone is sleeping
Grief is a house where no one can protect you
where the younger sister
will grow older than the older one
where the doors
no longer let you in
or out

(Found under a stone in Gram's garden.)

At night,
when we were little,
we tented Bailey's covers,
crawled underneath with our flashlights
and played cards: Hearts,
Whist, Crazy Eights,
and our favorite: Bloody Knuckles.
The competition was vicious.
All day, every day,

we were the Walker Girls—
two peas in a pod
thick as thieves—
but when Gram closed the door
for the night,
we bared our teeth.
We played for chores,
for slave duty,
for truths and dares and money.
We played to be better, brighter,
to be more beautiful,
more,
just more.
But it was all a ruse—
we played
so we could fall asleep
in the same bed
without having to ask,
so we could wrap together
like a braid,
so while we slept
our dreams could switch bodies.

(Found written on the inside cover of *Wuthering Heights*,
Lennie's room.)

My Father's Voice
by Tom Romano

TRY THIS (as quickly and as specifically as you can for 2–3 minutes)

✦ Write out anything that this piece brings to mind for you.

✦ As Tom Romano says in his book *Write What Matters* (2015), quote words you've never forgotten from someone who matters to you. With description and information, flesh out memory, following meaning. Bring to life a voice, a character, a time, a place.

✦ Borrow any line from this vignette, letting the line lead your thinking.

I remember my father calling my name on summer evenings when I was a boy in the late 1950s in northeastern Ohio. With neighborhood kids I played whiffle ball in the yard behind Doc Stires' office. Night fell fast, and sweat dried cold on the back of our necks. Stars appeared in the darkening sky. Lightning bugs pulsed a few feet off the ground. It was a magic time without daylight when a whiffle ball moved like a Whitey Ford fastball.

We had all promised to be home before nightfall, but no one was willing to break the spell. We played on with shouts and giddiness at the futility of catching and hitting in the growing dark. We knew in our bones that there was something more important going on than the game. No one wanted to let it go. Our play was summer and friendship and a tad of rebellion to be outside in the descending night beyond the time our parents wanted us home.

The first call came: my father's voice, short, booming, unmistakable, "Tom!" My father's voice. No trace in it of an Italian accent. He had been in America since 1914 when he left Nola, a village near Naples, he then a child of nine. My father's voice, still strong at 54-years-old, calling from behind the screen door at the top of the fire escape on the porch of our apartment over his tavern and bowling alleys. . . . My father's voice rising into the night sky, carrying over rooftops, alley, and neighbors' yards to land in my ears where I played with friends in the yard behind Doc Stires' office.

I ran all the way home—took twenty seconds, thirty tops. I reached the fire escape and looked up. My father's figure did not darken the screen door, but warm yellow light emanated from the apartment. He had worked hard to be successful in America. And like the Italian accent he left behind as a young learner of English, he also left behind much of his ethnicity.

I once asked an uncle of mine—Gigi Chiavari—my father's brother-in-law who lived to be 93, why he had come to America when he was 18. "Why I come 'cross?" Uncle Gigi said. "Same reason everybody come 'cross. You make a better living, a better home, a better life."

That's what my father had done. It has been many years since I've heard my father's voice. But writing this, I hear it now: My father's voice at twilight on a summer evening in small town America. My father's voice calling me home.

No!
by Julia F.

Your strong body
Slams against the floor
As you tumble
Down
Weak with grief
Your cries
Beg forgiveness and empathy
I am
So still
So calm
So quiet
I can hear your teardrops
Hit the cold, tiled floor

Your moment of sadness
Painful, genuine, and true
Stands framed in my mind
By the white door on which you lean
And the shake of her head
As she whispers a single word that
Hurls all of the world's power at you
No, she says
No!
After that
I don't remember
The sound of the door
Closing
Behind you
Knowing that this moment would come
Or the rumbling of your engine
As you drove away
Only to return on weekends
And never
When I need you

TRY THIS (as quickly and as specifically as you can for 2–3 minutes)

+ Write out anything that Julia's piece brings to mind for you.

+ Borrow any line or phrase from this poem, letting the line lead your thinking.

© 2018 by Linda Rief from *The Quickwrite Handbook: 100 Mentor Texts to Jumpstart Your Students' Thinking and Writing*. Portsmouth, NH: Heinemann.

TRY THIS (as quickly and as specifically as you can for 2–3 minutes)

+ Write out anything this poem brings to mind for you.

+ Borrow any line and write off or from that line, letting the line lead your thinking.

+ Whose picture sits on "your desk"? What does that picture bring to mind for you?

+ This writer implies that his grandfather did more for him than his father ever did. He was closer to his grandfather. Describe the ways in which a relationship you have, or had with someone, is different from the expected one.

Norman Moskowitz
by Mel Glenn

My grandfather's picture sits on my desk

While I do my homework.

My father spent money on me.

My grandfather spent time.

As I struggle with trig and other responsibilities

I remember how my grandfather would

Take me for walks in the park,

Explain how a screwball was thrown,

Encourage me to think well of myself.

I really don't want to wrestle with world history,

The gross national product and Nathaniel Hawthorne.

I just want to go to the park with you again, Grandpa.

Excerpt from *Aristotle and Dante Discover the Secrets of the Universe*
by Benjamin Alire Sáenz

One summer night I fell asleep, hoping the world would be different when I woke. In the morning, when I opened my eyes, the world was the same. I threw off the sheets and lay there as the heat poured in through the open window.

My hand reached for the dial on the radio. "Alone" was playing. Crap. "Alone," a song by a group called Heart. Not my favorite song. Not my favorite group. Not my favorite topic. "You don't know how long . . ."

I was fifteen. I was bored. I was miserable.

As far as I was concerned, the sun could have melted the blue right off the sky. Then the sky would be as miserable as I was.

TRY THIS (as quickly and as specifically as you can for 2–3 minutes)

+ Write out anything this excerpt brings to mind for you.

+ Borrow any line and let the line lead your thinking (for example, "One summer night," "I was— any age—I was bored. I was miserable," or "As far as I was concerned").

Paul Hewitt

by Mel Glenn

TRY THIS (as quickly and as
specifically as you can for 2–3
minutes)

+ Write out anything this poem
  brings to mind for you.
+ Borrow any line from which
  to write, letting the line lead
  your thinking.
+ In what ways do you agree
  or disagree with what this
  student is saying about
  teaching, or what this student
  feels is important to learn?

Please, sir, I don't mean to be disrespectful.

I did raise my hand.

I mean, who cares if Macbeth becomes a monster,

If Huck Finn rescues Jim,

If Willie Loman never finds happiness?

They're just characters in books.

What have they got to do with me?

I mean, I'm never going hunting for white whales.

I'm never going to fight in the Civil War.

And I certainly don't live in the Dust Bowl.

Tell me instead how to

Make money, pick up girls.

Then maybe I'll listen.

You got any books that deal with real life?

© 2018 by Linda Rief from *The Quickwrite Handbook: 100 Mentor Texts to Jumpstart Your Students' Thinking and Writing.* Portsmouth, NH: Heinemann.

Reply to the Question: "How Can You Become a Poet?"

by Eve Merriam

take the leaf of a tree

trace its exact shape

the outside edges

and inner lines

memorize the way it is fastened to the twig

(and how the twig arches from the branch)

how it springs forth in April

how it is panoplied in July

by late August

crumple it in your hand

so that you smell its end-of-summer sadness

chew its woody stem

listen to its autumn rattle

watch it as it atomizes in the November air

then in winter

when there is no leaf left

invent one

TRY THIS (as quickly and as specifically as you can for 2–3 minutes)

+ Think of an ordinary object from nature or from your life. Something you care about. Look closely (in your mind) at the object. Write out what you see, smell, feel. Write using the second-person pronoun *you* as being understood in the poem.

+ Borrow any line, write it down, and let the line lead your thinking.

+ Notice how the poet stretches out time by using the months April, July, August, or the seasons autumn and winter. Stretch out what you notice about your object over time.

Interlude

In "How Can You Become a Poet?" Eve Merriam writes about an object. Catherine Flynn, a teacher and blogger, used Merriam's poem to write about an experience.

Reply to the Question: "How Can You Become a Poet?"
by Catherine Flynn

Sit by a crackling fire,
Under a star-filled sky,
The air alive
With the song of crickets
And tree frogs
Thrumming and trilling
   Idgit   idgit
Idgit   idgit
   Idgit   idgit
Let their music seep
Into your soul.
Study the flames,
Leaping and licking
At a teepee of logs,
Illuminating the night.

Be dazzled
By sparks,
Orange fireflies
Dancing and swirling,
Tracing a glowing trail
As they race toward the heavens.

When I read Merriam's and Flynn's poems to my students, I read them as a pair, pointing out that Merriam writes about an object, while Flynn writes about an experience. I invite them to think about an object and/or an experience and "look closely" at either or both through their writing. Months later I thought of Chatherine Flynn's poem as I stepped out onto our deck to watch an eclipse. When I came back in, I wrote:

> *Stand on your deck in the dark—look toward the east at the full moon as she rises over Little Bay—listen to the sounds of the night—a train whistle as it approaches the Durham station—the bark of a distant coyote—wonder where the doe is with her three fawns—watch carefully as the first dark shadow washes across the face of the moon—*

For some reason I keep going back to these words and add to them again and again. Perhaps a prose poem? Perhaps a moment for a fictional character? Perhaps an interlude in a memoir piece? The importance is, I've captured something when and if I can ever use it.

Notice what Jacob wrote in his writer's-reader's notebook as a quickwrite in response to the poems by Eve Merriam and Catherine Flynn:

Pack carefully. Bring the glove, re-laced and conditioned countless times. Bring the bat, covered with scuffs and the pants you never wash. Bring the hat stained with sweat. Bring the uniform that kept your team together. Bring the passion for the game.

This quickwrite remained in his notebook for a few weeks with no further development. That's fine.

About six weeks later, after we read an article by Rick Bragg entitled "Skeleton Plunges Face-First Back into the Olympic Games," an article Ralph Fletcher shared with me, I asked the students to write down a line from the article that stuck with them. Jacob wrote: "If you are clumsy and make a mistake, there is pain and often blood." We talked about what we noticed about the article. In his notebook, Jacob wrote this: "Descriptions

TEACHER NOTE Notice that this interlude is different from so many others. I wanted you to see the entire process Jacob went through to craft his piece "Dinger" (see p. 82) from quickwrite to best piece. These two quickwrites, which sat in Jacob's writer's-reader's notebook for weeks, eventually became the impetus for a personal essay. He used not only the quickwrite but some of the craft moves he noticed from Rick Bragg. Keep in mind, also, he read this piece in draft to me and received feedback. I pointed out what he did well, asked him questions I had, and made a suggestion or two before he went to final draft. Students need our feedback in process and they need time to look back at various chunks of writing that feed into bigger pieces.

we are able to relate to. Dialogue used to up the ante. Metaphor—comparison to known object. Repetition—picture this, picture this, etc."

I asked the students to look carefully at one particular paragraph in the article and to write it down in their writer's-reader's notebooks. Jacob copied: "There is no affectation here, no baggy pants and thrash music like snowboarders have, no ice skaters sequins and storied history, no cinematic skiing glory acted out by a rugged Robert Redford, as in the downhill."

We talked about this particular craft move: *describing something by what it was not.* I asked the students to look back through their notebooks to some writing about an experience and to try and describe it that same way, *by what it was not.* Jacob went all the way back to September to a baseball experience and wrote:

> There is no game winning shot here. No buzzer beaters and running out clocks. No special plays or pre-determined routes, No penalty kicks, No flops, Nobody you have to blame, there is no consistency. There is no assurance, nothing here is ever the same. There is only surprise.

Dinger
by Jacob F.

Make sure to pack carefully: Bring the glove, re-laced and conditioned countless times to keep it pristine. Bring the bat, covered with scuffs and dents from previous seasons, each dent with a story to tell. Bring the pants you never wash, to preserve its luck. Bring the knee-high socks that shrink and cling to your shins, as soon as you get hit by the summer sun. Bring the hat, stained with sweat from tournaments and championships. Bring the cleats, the trusty New Balances that withstood singles, doubles, triples and homeruns. Bring the uniform that kept your team together, with the lingering scent of artificially flavored sunflower seeds. Bring the passion for the game.

© 2018 by Linda Rief from *The Quickwrite Handbook: 100 Mentor Texts to Jumpstart Your Students' Thinking and Writing.* Portsmouth, NH: Heinemann.

The game . . . there is no game-winning shot here, no three-pointers or flops. There are no penalty kick or headers. There are no power plays, cheap shots, or glove saves. There is no one-handed catch or tackle that gets the crowd roaring.

There is only surprise; no play is exactly the same. There are home plate celebrations, collisions and walk-off hits. There are diving grabs in the outfield and double plays in the infield. There are runners, sometimes sliding in safely below a cloud of dirt and sometimes being slapped on the leg before wearily jogging back to the dugout. There are wild pitches and passed balls. There is suspense, there is always a question in your head and a split second you have to react, move accordingly and keep the ball in front of you.

This isn't tee-ball, this isn't coach-pitch, this isn't your average town league. In fact, it isn't your town league at all. These are teams, great teams. From all over the United States. Gathered in an historic baseball community known as Cooperstown, New York. One hundred and four teams have seven days to make countless memories.

Memories to take back home with you. Pack carefully: Take the glove, now stained with the golden brown sand from the infield of stadium two. Take the bat, that helped you with a game-tying and game-winning hit, now with even more scuffs to look back on. Take the pants you will never wear again, because your coach forced you to wash them, as they were stinking up the cabins.

Take the knee high socks, that are supposedly "one size fits all" and slid down your leg while taking a turn at first and sprinting for second. Take the hat that barely fit on your head on the first day, but now has a perfectly tailored fit. Take the cleats that still have Cooperstown sand inside the sole, with broken laces and a stench coming from seven well-fought games. Take the uniform, the number seven on your back and the Cooperstown logo on the front, soon to be framed and never touched again.

Most importantly, take the baseball. No longer a snowy white and no longer a perfect sphere. The ball that jumped off the bat, over the fence, retrieved by a young boy who also hopes to play on these fields and given back to you, the boy rounding the bases as your teammates scream from the dugout, "Dinger."

© 2018 by Linda Rief from *The Quickwrite Handbook: 100 Mentor Texts to Jumpstart Your Students' Thinking and Writing*. Portsmouth, NH: Heinemann.

TRY THIS (as quickly and as specifically as you can for 2–3 minutes)

+ Write all that this poem brings to mind for you.

+ Think of a time you did something you probably should not have done, but did it to impress someone else. You might want to take Ralph Fletcher's advice: start at the "waterfall" (*jump* right into the scene—pun intended).

+ Borrow any line and write off or from that line, letting the line lead your thinking ("I was second to chickenest," "I'd never done this," "my mother'd kill me if she knew," "I didn't dare think," etc.).

Swinging the River
by Charles Harper Webb

One by one they climbed out on the thickest limb,
crouched like 12-year-old Tarzans, then
jumped, whipped through needley branches,
strangling the hemp rope till their nerve broke
and they dropped thirty feet to the river.

I was second-to-last in line. Second-
to-chickenest, I guessed. I'd never done this.

Rocks and tricky currents had drowned two kids
in three years. (One was never found.)
My mother'd kill me if she knew. . . .

My turn. My shaking hands grabbed at the rope.
I didn't dare think, just jumped,
swooped down, arced up, higher, flew free,
seemed to hang in the air while the splash
reached up to swallow me, blacking out

the sun, the feathery pine trees,
the blonde girl on the bank
whose wet shirt showed her swelling nipples
who'd said hi the day before,
who was here with her aunt for two short weeks.

I sank like an anvil. Colder and colder.
I quietly gave up hope. Then my feet
touched a dead kid. Slime-hands
clutched at me. I kicked wildly
into sickening ooze, broke free, went shooting up

through millions of bubbles, rocketing out
into the blonde girl's smile.

The Cat

by Lynn S. Adams

"Drown them before you get attached," my dad used to be famous for saying. He meant anything—children, kittens, emotions—just another way he tried to show a tough exterior to the world. My first glimpse into the true fragility and depth of emotion underneath his armor came when I was a child.

I remember when I had the opportunity to finally have my own pet. A stray cat had wandered into the neighborhood when I was eight or nine years old. Our dog had recently been hit by a UPS man (an experience that did leave me scarred for a long time—as my younger brother put it: "the gift man hit my dog"). I was ready for a pet of my own.

"Don't name her," he said. So my brothers and I timidly called her "Miss Kitty" (it was not *really* a name).

"Don't feed her," he demanded. I'm not sure how long that lasted, but it wasn't long. I think my mother had a coupon for Meow Mix. We started leaving a bowl out back near the patio sliding doors. I recall staying up at night, crying, listening to my dad tell my mom how much he didn't want *that cat*. I prayed he would change his mind, but I think now it was always changed.

"Don't let her in," he commanded, one of the first times when I saw my father's gruff, rough exterior crack. . . . Later that winter, he lay on the couch on a lazy Sunday after snow-blowing the driveway during one of the numerous snowstorms upstate New York had to offer. I entered the family room, a football game on the TV. My dad was under an afghan knit by my mom, Miss Kitty snoozing on his chest.

"Don't move her," he murmured.

TRY THIS (as quickly and as specifically as you can for 2–3 minutes)

- Write out anything this piece brings to mind for you.

- Think of a time someone was adamant about you not getting a pet and show how that person changed or did not change his or her mind.

- Notice how Adams uses dialogue to show the slow change in her dad's attitude toward the cat. Try using dialogue in the same way for a character or person you are writing about.

TEACHER NOTE Showing a person and the change in that person through dialogue is a craft move you might want to point out to your students after they have done a quickwrite.

© 2018 by Linda Rief from *The Quickwrite Handbook: 100 Mentor Texts to Jumpstart Your Students' Thinking and Writing.* Portsmouth, NH: Heinemann.

TRY THIS (as quickly and as specifically as you can for 2–3 minutes)

+ Write out all that comes to mind when you think "roller coaster."

+ Borrow the line "It starts with the climbing in," "at the top, out on the edge," "in the eyes-shut, heart-stopped drop," or any other line that resonates with you, letting the line lead your thinking.

Roller Coaster
by Ginger Murchison

It starts with the climbing in,

nerved-up enough

for that defiance

of gravity, the slow-grind

rackety-clack one-inch cog

at a time—the mystery of machinery,

the sane and safe weightedness

of stiff-starched values,

wondering if there were

sins we'd committed

since our last confession, then

at the top, out on the edge,

beyond the solid-ground world

parents live in, test life,

theirs and our own, up where

we are a hole in the sky,

wholly abandoned in the eyes-

shut, heart-stopped drop,

like lawlessness on falling's

crisp speed, the first curve, a blur,

the world's suddenness,

metal, air and a prayer

half-mouthed, spun,

flung into another plunge,

a curve swerving,

a tiny boat in a tempest—

and isn't this how we want

to live, live higher up,

hungry to leave the ground,

flinging sparks, the lights brighter,

the dark darker, bodies at war

with mere air, but still obedient

to the tracks laid down

to keep us on track.

© 2018 by Linda Rief from *The Quickwrite Handbook: 100 Mentor Texts to Jumpstart Your Students' Thinking and Writing.* Portsmouth, NH: Heinemann.

TRY THIS (as quickly and as specifically as you can for 2–3 minutes)

✦ Consider the phrase *morning light.* Write about an experience that comes to mind, capturing especially the sights and sounds.

✦ Hunter writes of a fishing experience, which often begins in morning light. What's an experience you've had, maybe only once, or often, that involves morning light?

✦ His experience with tuna fishing is often unsuccessful, although they keep persisting. Write out what his fishing experience brings to mind for you, something you go at again and again, successfully or unsuccessfully.

✦ Borrow any line from which to write. Let the line guide your thinking.

Today's Catch
by Hunter R.

Three am. Roll out of bed. Eat a quick breakfast. Get in the car, and head to the dock. As the engines grind to life I crawl onto the boat. Rolling waves crash against her side. The boat rocks to life, and I stagger my way to the bow to find stable seating.

The waves grow bigger, launching the white caps higher into the sky, like mini-volcanoes that suppress themselves under the waves. I look out. Ocean as far as the eye can see. An unbelievable view—morning light— purple, pink, orange, and gold rising from the sea. It reminds me of the poem "Nothing Gold Can Stay," by Robert Frost. I wish it would stay like that forever, but in an instant, it is gone.

The stench of dead fish rolls by as we pass a fishing vessel. Fish lurk underneath their boat in blood-drenched water from the ship. Whales lunge for the sky and crash in a tremendous splash of waves.

When we reach the Isle of Shoals, we drop lines for mackerel. The fish catch our hooks as if we are using a net. They pile up in overflowing buckets that pour over the edge, fish flopping for their lives as their gills search for water.

When we have caught enough mackerel to last us through the day for bait, we head out; after an hour of driving we reach our spot. While others set the tuna lines, I drop my own line, trying to avoid the gut-wrenching feeling of seasickness. It never tends to bother me when I'm doing something. Fishing keeps me busy.

About eight in the morning the fish-finder bleeps. "Beep . . . beep . . . beep . . . ZZZzzzz!"

"We're on!" my dad screams, as the line zips out with a 300-pound drag. "Anchor off, start the engines," he yells. The fish drags the line out before the engines are even started.

Time goes by too fast. Everything is rushed. In panic. In excitement. After a long hard fight of pull and drag, drag and pull, we realize it's a shark. A seven-foot blue shark. A disappointment. Can't sell it. Can't eat it. Up against the boat, the shark breaks loose, and we reset the lines in hopes for a tuna.

Remembrance
For My Grandmother
Clarice Smith Chapman, 1914–1989
by Lindsay O.

I remember . . . we collected wild strawberries

And made mud pies and built

Block houses and guided

Our cart down the supermarket aisle

And picked carrots and washed

Dishes and baked cookies and cut

Paper dolls and watched chickadees

And played checkers and ate scrambled eggs and

Took our time on the stairs

And you never told me you were dying.

I wanted the chance to say goodbye.

© 2018 by Linda Rief from *The Quickwrite Handbook: 100 Mentor Texts to Jumpstart Your Students' Thinking and Writing.* Portsmouth, NH: Heinemann.

TRY THIS (as quickly and as specifically as you can for 2–3 minutes)

+ Think of someone you care deeply about (who might still be alive). Using Lindsay's phrase "I remember . . . we" and her style linking one thing to another, write out the things you have done with this person.

+ Write in the same way using the second-person *you* instead of *we*.

+ Borrow any line and write as quickly as you can all that the line brings to mind.

+ Write about whatever this poem brings to mind for you.

TEACHER NOTE You might ask your students to think about the way Lindsay links everything with "and . . . and . . . and . . . ." What does that craft move show us about the relationship? Notice also how Lindsay moves from more physical movements to more sedentary movements. What does that show a reader?

TRY THIS (as quickly and as specifically as you can for 2–3 minutes)

✦ Write out anything that this poem brings to mind for you.

✦ Borrow any line, letting the line lead your thinking.

✦ Change the first line of Kearney's poem to two of anything: "I have two siblings," "I have two fathers," "I have four sets of grandparents," "I have no friends."

✦ Sometimes people have to make hard choices in their lives: divorce, moving, breaking up friendships, putting an elderly relative in assisted living. Kearney asks a difficult question: "What kind of love is that?" What hard questions have you asked yourself in response to hard choices you've made? What are some hard choices others have made for you? In what ways did you accept or reject those choices?

Two Mothers
by Meg Kearney

I have two mothers
but not like Toshi
who has two mothers

who live with her
in New Hook and brag
about how much

she looks like one
and acts like
the other. I have two

mothers, but only
know the second
one. My first
mother loved me

so much
she gave me away.
I wonder if it bothers

my mother, the one
who took me in, that
I don't look like her.

I wonder if she ever
worries that my other
mother will want me
back. I wonder if she
ever thinks of me, my
other mother. I hope

no one ever loves me
as much as she did.
What kind of love is that?

'Til the Stars Burn Out
by Ryan W.

We fish 'til we are out of bait.

Play soccer 'til we can't feel our feet.

Look for sand dollars 'til the beach is empty.

We play capture the flag 'til the sun goes down.

Catch minnows 'til our bucket is full.

Do gridiron 'til the season is over.

We play football 'til we own the end zone.

Build with k'nex 'til the boxes are empty.

Watch sports 'til our eyes droop.

We play whiffle ball 'til we can't see in the night sky.

Ride bikes 'til we can't peddle any more.

Play racquetball 'til arms feel like rubber.

Wrestle 'til we fall down exhausted.

Play Wii 'til our fingers fall off.

Ski 'til we get frostbite.

Vacation together 'til we are sick of each other.

We lie outside and watch the stars 'til the sun comes up.

We are

Best friends for life.

TRY THIS (as quickly and as specifically as you can for 2–3 minutes)

+ Write out anything that Ryan's poem brings to mind for you.

+ Borrow any line from the poem, letting the line lead your thinking.

+ Write out all that you and your best friend do together.

Baseball

by John Updike

It looks easy from a distance,

easy and lazy, even,

until you stand up to the plate

and see the fastball sailing inside,

an inch from your chin,

or circle in the outfield

straining to get a bead

on a small black dot

a city block or more high,

a dark star that could fall

on your head like a leaden meteor.

The grass, the dirt, the deadly hops

between your feet and overeager glove:

football can be learned,

and basketball finessed, but

there is no hiding from baseball

the fact that some are chosen

and some are not—those whose mitts

feel too left-handed,

who are scared at third base

of the pulled line drive,

and at first base are scared

of the shortstop's wild throw

that stretches you out like a gutted deer.

TRY THIS (as quickly and as specifically as you can for 2–3 minutes)

✦ Write about anything this poem brings to mind for you.

✦ Write about something that looked easy but actually is not.

✦ Borrow the line "it looks easy from a distance" or any other line, letting the line lead your thinking.

There is nowhere to hide when the ball's
spotlight swivels your way,
and the chatter around you falls still,
and the mothers on the sidelines,
your own among them, hold their breaths,
and you whiff on a terrible pitch
or in the infield achieve
something with the ball so
ridiculous you blush for years.
It's easy to do. Baseball was
invented in America, where beneath
the good cheer and sly jazz the chance
of failure is everybody's right,
beginning with baseball.

© 2018 by Linda Rief from *The Quickwrite Handbook: 100 Mentor Texts to Jumpstart Your Students' Thinking and Writing*. Portsmouth, NH: Heinemann.

TRY THIS (as quickly and as specifically as you can for 2–3 minutes)

- Write anything the excerpts from this book bring to mind for you.

- Write about a time you might have felt isolated from the world: Where were you? Why were you there? What was it like there?

- Write your own list of things you would love to do, that for whatever reason, you have never had the chance to do.

- Madeline has a computer and windows in her room, so she is exposed to an outside world, yet has never experienced what she sees and hears. It's almost impossible to imagine being a "bubble baby," but if you were, what would you be longing for, what would you miss from the outside world? In other words, what are the sights, sounds, tastes, smells, and touches that you love the most? (Think in terms of one experience: riding a dirt bike, playing baseball, playing a trumpet, jumping from a rope swing, making cookies, etc.)

Excerpt from *Everything, Everything*
by Nicola Yoon

What if you couldn't touch anything in the outside world? Never breathe in the fresh air, feel the sun warm your face . . . or kiss the boy next door? In *Everything, Everything*, Madeline is a girl who's literally allergic to the outside world, and Olly is the boy who moves in next door . . . and becomes the greatest risk she's ever taken. (Amazon Book Summary)

My disease is as rare as it is famous. Basically, I'm allergic to the world. It's a form of Severe Combined Immunodeficiency. Basically, I'm allergic to the world. Anything could trigger a bout of sickness. It could be the chemicals in the cleaner used to wipe the table that I just touched. . . . It could be the exotic spice of the food I just ate. . . . No one knows the triggers, but everyone knows the consequences. According to my mom, I almost died as an infant. So I stay on SCID row. I don't leave my house, have not left my house in seventeen years.

I've read many more books than you. It doesn't matter how many you've read. I've read more. Believe me, I've had the time.

In my white room, against my white walls, on my glistening white bookshelves, book spines provide the only color. They come to me from Outside, decontaminated and vacuum-sealed in plastic wrap.

Maddy writes her name in the books, in case they get lost, which she knows will never happen because no one is allowed to visit her—except her mother and Carla, her nurse. Still, she writes her name in each book with a list of "Reward if Found." These are some of her wishful rewards:

- Picnic with me in a pollen-filled field of poppies, lilies, and endless man-in-the-moon marigolds under a clear blue summer sky.
- Drink tea with me in a lighthouse in the middle of the Atlantic Ocean in the middle of a hurricane.
- Snorkel with me off Molokini to spot the Hawaiian state fish— the humuhumunukunukuapuaa.

Excerpt from
Love, Hate & Other Filters
By Samira Ahmed

. . . There's a steady flow of news and innuendo, and it's hard to discern the truth.

I'm frozen. My fingers curl tightly around my phone.

The entire room is in chaos, but I see the action as if through the blades of a whirring fan. Disjointed and surreal. My stomach lurches.

A terrorist attack. Another tragedy. Is there no end? Is this how life will always be? I want to know more, but there is one piece of information I absolutely hope I don't hear. I whisper a prayer to the universe. "Please, please let everyone be okay. Please don't let it be a Muslim."

I know I'm not the only one hoping for this. I know millions of American Muslims—both religious and secular—are echoing these very same words at this very moment. I know I'm not a very good Muslim, but I hope my prayers are heard. Prayers for the dead and wounded. Prayers for ourselves. Prayers for peace, hoping that no more lives are lost to hate.

I'm scared. I'm not just scared that somehow I'll be next; it's a quieter fear and more insidious. I'm scared of the next Muslim ban. I'm scared of my dad getting pulled into Secondary Security Screening at the airport for "random" questioning. I'm scared some of the hijabi girls I know will get their scarves pulled off while they're walking down the sidewalk—or worse. I'm scared of being the object of fear and loathing and suspicion again. Always.

TRY THIS (as specifically and as quickly as you can for 2–3 minutes)

+ Write out anything this excerpt brings to mind for you, either from a personal standpoint or in any way connected to the world you know today or in the past.

+ Borrow any line, letting the line lead your thinking and your writing.

+ Write out those things that scare or frighten you about the world today.

Beyond Self

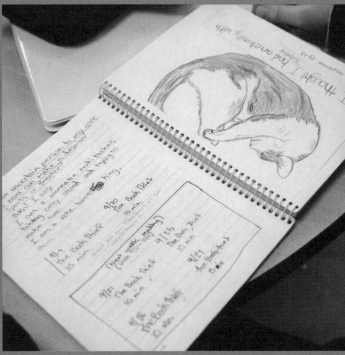

Cities
By Catherine P.

Hundreds of cars pack the streets,
Horns blaring,
Drivers screeching,
And tires squealing.

Enormous buildings tower above me,
Reaching for the stars,
Leaping for the moon,
Scraping the sky.

Thousands of people press against me,
Chatting on cell phones,
Hailing taxis,
Lugging filled-to-the-brim shopping bags.

"There are hundreds of things to do in a city,"
my mother tells me.
"And millions already doing them,"
I retort.

© 2018 by Linda Rief from *The Quickwrite Handbook: 100 Mentor Texts to Jumpstart Your Students' Thinking and Writing*. Portsmouth, NH: Heinemann.

TRY THIS (as specifically and as quickly as you can for 2–3 minutes)

✦ Write down anything this poem brings to mind for you.

✦ Borrow any phrase or line, letting the line lead your thinking as you write.

✦ Instead of the city, describe the country or some other location that holds significance for you.

✦ Describe the city or any other place that lets the reader know how much you like or dislike the place from the way you describe it.

✦ There are often two points of view to any place. Try describing that same place you described from the opposite point of view.

TEACHER NOTE Catherine's mother tries to convince her daughter that the city is worth the noise and crowds. It is in her last line that she captures what she really thinks about the city. Have your students play with their first draft writing, trying to capture their stance toward a place in their last line or two. For contrast, you could also pair this poem with Allan DeFina's poem "When a City Leans Against the Sky" in his book by the same title.

The Husband
by Joseph Mills

He comes every day to eat lunch and sit
with her in the sun room. Sometimes he reads
letters out loud from their children or friends;
sometimes he reads the paper as she sleeps.
One day the staff makes her favorite cake
to celebrate their anniversary,
and he tells how, to buy her ring, he worked
months of overtime at the factory,
so she thought he was seeing someone else.
"As if I would look at other women
when I have Pearl," he says, shaking his head.
She begins to cry and tells him, "You're sweet,
but I miss my husband." He pats her hand.
"I know," he says. "It's all right. Try some cake."

TRY THIS (as quickly and as specifically as you can for 2–3 minutes)

+ Write down anything this poem brings to mind for you. It could be a feeling of sadness or love that you've experienced that comes through in a similar, single moment.

+ As you read, you might be reminded of a grandparent or neighbor whose memory is slipping. Write out a moment or scene when you realized this was happening.

+ Borrow any line and let the line lead your thinking. It could be "He comes every day" or any other line.

© 2018 by Linda Rief from *The Quickwrite Handbook: 100 Mentor Texts to Jumpstart Your Students' Thinking and Writing.* Portsmouth, NH: Heinemann.

Traveling Through the Dark
by William Stafford

Traveling through the dark I found a deer
dead on the edge of the Wilson River road.
It is usually best to roll them into the canyon:
that road is narrow; to swerve might make more dead.

By glow of the tail-light I stumbled back of the car
and stood by the heap, a doe, a recent killing;
she had stiffened already, almost cold.
I dragged her off; she was large in the belly.

My fingers touching her side brought me the reason—
her side was warm; her fawn lay there waiting,
alive, still, never to be born.
Beside that mountain road I hesitated.

The car aimed ahead its lowered parking lights;
Under the hood purred the steady engine.
I stood in the glare of the warm exhaust turning red;
around our group I could hear the wilderness listen.

I thought hard for us all—my only swerving—,
Then pushed her over the edge into the river.

TRY THIS (as quickly and as specifically as you can for 2–3 minutes)

+ Write out anything this poem brings to mind for you.

+ Borrow any line and let the line lead your thinking.

+ Stafford's last two lines imply that the decision he made was difficult. In what way have you, or anyone around you, had to make a difficult decision? Describe what happened. What made it difficult? What made it the right decision? Or the wrong decision?

TEACHER NOTE This is a wonderful poem that leads to a lot of discussion as to why he made that decision and could have or could not have done anything differently. Students had to look into the poem again and again to find the reasons to support their thinking.

Excerpt from *The Boys in the Boat*
by Daniel James Brown

There is a thing that sometimes happens in rowing that is hard to achieve and hard to define. Many crews, even winning crews, never really find it. Others find it but can't sustain it. It's called "swing." It only happens when all eight oarsmen are rowing in such perfect unison that no single action by any one is out of synch with those of all the others. It's not just that the oars enter and leave the water at precisely the same instant. Sixteen arms must begin to pull, sixteen knees must begin to fold and unfold, eight bodies must begin to slide forward and backward, eight backs must bend and straighten all at once. Each minute action—each subtle turning of wrists—must be mirrored exactly by each oarsman, from one end of the boat to the other. Only then will the boat continue to run, unchecked, fluidly and gracefully between pulls of the oars. Only then will it feel as if the boat is a part of each of them, moving as if on its own. Only then does pain entirely give way to exultation. Rowing then becomes a kind of perfect language. Poetry, that's what a good swing feels like.

TRY THIS (as quickly and as specifically as you can for 2–3 minutes)

✦ Write out anything this excerpt brings to mind for you.

✦ Borrow any line or phrase from which to write, letting the line lead your thinking.

✦ Think about an activity in which you participate as a team that has its own kind of "swing," where the pain gives way to exultation. Describe that activity.

✦ Think about an activity in which you participate on your own. What is there about the activity that is "hard to achieve and hard to define"? Try describing that thing. (It could be a sport, playing an instrument, drawing, even writing or reading.) Start with Brown's line, "There is a thing that happens in ____."

Just a Runner
by Kylee D. E.

There's something magical about putting on my running shoes. I can feel the thrill and excitement of my legs preparing for a workout, and the shoes sending twinges of energy up to my muscles. I'm pumped. I feel this want, this need, to just spring up and run forever.

At first, my muscles start to warm up, and get used to working. Then I feel that burning pain that acts as my fuel to keep me going. This pain is like no other. It gives me a sense of euphoria, and drives me to push harder. It isn't sharp, but is a strong sensation that gives me a boost, and lets me know that I'm pushing myself to the limit. As opposed to a sharp cramp, I can endure this pain. I love it. I don't know what I would do without it. It makes me feel like I'm in control.

I'm in the midst of the rhythm that engulfs me, and I don't want it to leave. Muscles flex, lungs breathe. . . . Muscles flex, lungs breathe. . . . Muscles flex, lungs breathe. . . . This rhythm sends my mind away, floating and flitting from the tops of the trees to down below the ground. My mind is in a trance. It takes an extreme amount of willpower to resurface from this trance. Since I enjoy it, I don't want to leave it.

My legs are numb, not from exhaustion, but from repetition and strength. I don't feel the pain that much anymore. Quads pull, calves push. . . Quads pull, calves push. . . Quads pull, calves push. . . . My legs do what they have to do, and I can drift from cloud to cloud, tree to tree, and feel the freedom of happiness.

I'm just a runner. Just a runner. But really, I am someone who is so in love with this sport that when I'm in the middle of a trance, all cares leave me. I'm not aware of myself. I know I'm moving, and where I am, and who I am. But nothing else matters. I'm here, and doing what I love to do. Isn't that a person's goal in life? To be happy?

Some people don't understand that to make me happiest, all you have to do is let me go for a run. That's it. Nothing else can make me happier.

© 2018 by Linda Rief from *The Quickwrite Handbook: 100 Mentor Texts to Jumpstart Your Students' Thinking and Writing*. Portsmouth, NH: Heinemann.

TEACHER NOTE Kylee's piece, "Just a Runner," is a good example of what Daniel James Brown means by "swing," getting into the rhythm of something seamlessly, so completely involved in the activity that even the pain is painless. Notice some of the ways Kylee uses language in a way that reinforces her movements, the rhythm in the running.

Excerpt from *The Art of Racing in the Rain*
by Garth Stein

Gestures are all that I have; sometimes they must be grand in nature. And while I occasionally step over the line and into the world of the melodramatic, it is what I do in order to communicate clearly and effectively. In order to make my point understood without question. I have no words I can rely on because, much to my dismay, my tongue was designed long and flat and loose, and therefore, is a horribly ineffective tool for pushing food around my mouth while chewing, and an even less effective tool for making clever and complicated polysyllabic sounds that can be linked together to form sentences. And that's why I'm here now waiting for Denny to come home, he should be here soon, lying on the cool tiles of the kitchen floor in a puddle of my own urine.

TRY THIS (as specifically and as quickly as you can for 2–3 minutes)

+ Write out anything this excerpt brings to mind for you.
+ Borrow any line, letting the line lead your thinking.
+ Write from an animal's perspective, crafting one scene in which you imagine what the animal must be thinking.

Interlude

Toby
by Lydia W.

I see the cross-rail as my rider turns my head toward it. The bit suddenly pushes harder at my lips. I feel the tap of the crop on my withers. I'm not a good jumper, but I still heave myself over the cross-rail. I turn the corner and come around, my feet sending up little poofs of dust as I dodge the other horses. My ears flatten. I hate crowds. Blackjack takes his time, as usual. I'm shorter than he is, but I'm off the racetrack.

I jump again, several times. We keep going until my owner, Dawn, puts up the fence to a straightaway. It looms before me, higher than the cross-rail. My rider urges me forward, but I feel her nervousness. I can't make that jump. I come up to it and turn my nose away.

Although my rider falls hard on my neck, she quickly rights herself and manages to circle me. She sends me forward, urging me toward the fence. This time I'm frightened. I don't want to try and fail, hurt myself and her, or even face the humiliation. I turn away again.

This time she backs me up, no nonsense, and steers me around the jump. Dawn puts down one side of the straightaway. I clear it with ease, and come around again, as she puts the side back up. I think of my pride (I'm a thoroughbred, for goodness sake!) and with a huge effort heave myself up and over that jump.

I hit the ground, cantering from the momentum. I'm still alive. I didn't fall, or knock down the pole, and even though my rider is unbalanced, she is unhurt. As I turn for another try at the jump, my fear is mixed with a keen sense of pride.

TEACHER NOTE You might show your students Lydia's piece, explaining that it began in response to the excerpt from *The Art of Racing in the Rain* by Garth Stein. We talked about imagining what an animal might think or feel but can only communicate through gestures. This interlude is meant to show that students are not always writing from their own perspective. Note that Lydia still takes this through the process of choice, feedback, drafting, and redrafting to achieve the best draft.

Old Woman in Folding Chair
by Linda Rief

How sad you look,
old woman in folding chair.
Blueberry eyes buried in furrows
of sun-parched wrinkles. Sweater
buttoned loose
swaddling shoulders and arms
like a little boy's hugs.

Who are you waiting for,
old woman in folding chair?
Why haven't they come?

Hands, kissed with October's first frost,
sit limp
in a garden of blue and yellow,
pink and purple polyester.
Who are you waiting for,
old woman?
Why haven't they come?

Plastic pocketbook,
tightly clasped,
holding your life.
Tennis shoes
neatly tied.
Where are you going,
old woman?
How long will it take?

How soon will I be
old woman in folding chair?

9 Aug.
Portland, OR Art Museum.
"Old Woman in Folding Chair"
Duane Hanson
virtual reality artist

TRY THIS (as quickly and as specifically as you can for 2–3 minutes)

✦ Write out anything this poem brings to mind for you.

✦ Borrow any line, letting the line lead your thinking in any direction it wants to go.

✦ Think about the word *old*. Write down the images, sounds, and movements that come to mind for you, whether it's a person or object.

✦ Personify the word *old*. How does *old* move, talk, think? How does *old* look, feel?

✦ Who or what comes to mind when you think of aging and changing? Describe that person, place, or thing as fully as you can. What do you notice, see, hear, think, and feel?

TEACHER NOTE This poem began with a sketch, drawn while viewing a virtual reality exhibit by Duane Hanson at the Portland Art Museum in Oregon. As I sketched, I jotted down my thinking. Back and forth. Sketch, write. Sketch, write. Drawing relaxes the mind. On any field trip invite your students to find an object that intrigues them. Sketch and write. In the classroom use art postcards or any pictures that stimulate your students' thinking. Sketch and write.

TRY THIS (as quickly and as specifically as you can for 2–3 minutes)

+ Galloway's description of this city in Arrow's memory may be far from any memory you have of any place you have lived. What are the memories you have of places you have been or places you have seen that might have come to mind because of this excerpt?

+ Arrow's grandmother says, "There is more to life than ice cream." What does this bring to mind for you?

+ What thoughts or questions come to mind as you read this excerpt?

Excerpt from *The Cellist of Sarajevo*
by Steven Galloway

The sun has been up for half an hour, but the streets are mostly deserted. She encounters a few people as she moves down the hill and into the old town, but she doesn't make eye contact with them. She passes the remnants of a shop that once sold the best ice cream, and she remembers being a small girl with her grandmother on this street. She asked her grandmother to stop, in the pleading voice of a child used to getting her way, even though she'd just had some ice cream not an hour earlier. When her grandmother said no, Arrow let go of her hand and refused to continue. Her grandmother knelt down, took Arrow's face in her hands, and kissed her on the forehead.

"There is more to life than ice cream," she said.

Arrow wonders, as this memory fades, what she would give up for a scoop of ice cream today. All the money she has? Certainly. Her rifle? Maybe. The one remaining photograph of her grandmother? She shakes her head and increases her pace, denying her mind a chance to answer.

This is her favorite time of day. . . . The absence of shelling is almost music, and she imagines if she closed her eyes she could convince herself that she was walking through the streets of Sarajevo as it used to be. Almost. She knows that in the city of her memory she wasn't hungry, and she wasn't bruised, and her shoulder didn't bear the weight of a gun. In the city of her memory there were always people out at this time of morning, preparing for the day to come. They wouldn't be shut in like invalids, exhausted from another night of wondering if a shell was about to land on their house.

Political Cartoons

What's Wrong with His Hands?
by Erin Warren

A Real Ivory Necklace by Mia H.

Free Body Check-Ups by Trinity C.

Genderless Bathrooms by Aaron H.

TRY THIS (as specifically and as quickly as you can for 5–8 minutes)

+ Write down several local or worldwide issues you care about.

+ Sketch your opinion in stick figures and key words. Use this sketch to begin thinking of all the reasons you support a particular issue. This sketch could lead to a much more fully developed essay on the issue or topic about which you feel so strongly and could become a more polished political cartoon that supports your issue.

+ In what way do you agree or disagree with the stance taken in one of the issues in these political cartoons? Write out your position.

TEACHER NOTE Show your students some professionally drawn political cartoons, helping them notice how the artists use symbols, exaggeration, labels, analogy, and irony to present their opinions visually.

© 2018 by Linda Rief from *The Quickwrite Handbook: 100 Mentor Texts to Jumpstart Your Students' Thinking and Writing*. Portsmouth, NH: Heinemann.

TRY THIS (as quickly and as specifically as you can for 2–3 minutes)

+ Write out anything that this excerpt brings to mind for you.

+ If we actually had the ability to relinquish color, what would be the advantages? What would be the disadvantages?

+ In what ways do you think the ability to alter genes will have a positive effect on people's lives? In what ways might it be negative?

+ Try crafting a scene completely in dialogue—no narration. A scene that shows tension through strong feelings of disagreement.

Excerpt from *The Giver*
by Lois Lowry

"I'm right, then," The Giver said. "You're beginning to see the color red.

"There was a time, actually . . . when flesh was many different colors. That was before we went to Sameness.

"We've never completely mastered Sameness. I suppose the genetic scientists are still hard at work trying to work the kinks out. Hair like Fiona's must drive them crazy."

"Why can't everyone see them? Why did colors disappear?"

"We relinquished color when we relinquished sunshine and did away with differences. . . . We gained control of many things. But we had to let go of others."

"We shouldn't have!" said Jonas fiercely.

In Response to Executive Order 9066
by Dwight Okita

All Americans of Japanese Descent Must Report to Relocation Centers

Dear Sirs:
Of course I'll come. I've packed my galoshes
and three packets of tomato seeds. Denise calls them
love apples. My father says where we're going
they won't grow.
I am a fourteen-year-old girl with bad spelling
and a messy room. If it helps any, I will tell you
I have always felt funny using chopsticks
and my favorite food is hot dogs.
My best friend is a white girl named Denise—
we look at boys together. She sat in front of me
all through grade school because of our names:
O'Connor, Ozawa. I know the back of Denise's head very well.
I tell her she's going bald. She tells me I copy on tests.
We're best friends.
I saw Denise today in Geography class.
She was sitting on the other side of the room.
"You're trying to start a war," she said, "giving secrets
away to the Enemy. Why can't you keep your big
mouth shut?"
I didn't know what to say.
I gave her a packet of tomato seeds
and asked her to plant them for me, told her
when the first tomato ripened
she'd miss me.

© 2018 by Linda Rief from The Quickwrite Handbook: 100 Mentor Texts to Jumpstart Your Students' Thinking and Writing. Portsmouth, NH: Heinemann.

TRY THIS (as quickly and as specifically as you can for 2–3 minutes)

+ Write out whatever this letter/poem brings to mind for you.

+ Borrow any line, letting the line lead your thinking.

+ During World War II, all Americans of Japanese descent were forced into internment camps, in the belief they might be aiding the enemy—*because* they were of Japanese descent and *even if* they were American citizens. What does the idea of doing this bring to mind for you, especially in our world today?

+ In what ways would you agree or disagree with Executive Order 9066?

© 2018 by Linda Rief from *The Quickwrite Handbook: 100 Mentor Texts to Jumpstart Your Students' Thinking and Writing.* Portsmouth, NH: Heinemann.

TRY THIS (as quickly and as specifically as you can for 2–3 minutes)

+ Write out anything Katya's poem brings to mind for you.

+ Borrow any line, letting the line lead your thinking in any direction.

+ Katya's poem is a love letter to the brain, from a neuroscientist, someone who studies the brain. What organism or concept particular to another discipline, one that fascinates you, that holds your curiosity, could you write a love letter to? Write it. Let your letter show all you know and show your curiosity about all you don't know.

A Neuroscientist's Love Letter
by Katya E.

I know you are terrified.
Your brain trembles in your skull.
Intricate layers of matter
Cradle microscopic chaos,
And everywhere your neurotransmitters scream.
You are going to die, they say,
But don't shoot the messenger.
If I was the kind of person
You couldn't get out of your head,
I'd sprint through your synapses,
Crawl through every cortex,
Just to find the source of your
Misplaced adrenaline,
And tell your amygdala to leave
Your night alone.
You deserve more than fear.
If I was always on your mind,
I'd study the snowflake dendrites
Always reaching for an answer,
The way your neurons tell you that
Tomorrow could be even worse,
How they are just trying to do their job,
But like you, they tried too hard.
And not even the endless caverns of your cerebellum,
Not the nerve fibers bending in a quiet forest,
Not even the footprints of memory
Stamped in temporary permanence
All over your brain

TEACHER NOTE I had Katya as a student in eighth grade, a time during which she read and wrote a lot of poetry. This poem was written while she was a sophomore at Portsmouth Christian Academy. Katya knows I am a teacher who writes and that I want to be a writer who teaches. She wants to be a writer who practices psychology.

Are perfect.
But you are afraid. You say it's because
The night is too long, because you are
Not good enough, lonely or alone,
One of the two.
This is the truth,
This is why.
Your serotonin levels fell with the sky.
Adrenaline battled to compensate,
And now you're always running away.
This darkness through the window,
The shadow where torture hides?
It's a lack of endorphins, increase in epinephrine,
Compounded by an autonomic response.
Fight or flight, fight or flight,
Cries the organ that owns you.
But even if you're out of your mind,
I hope I'm still in the back of it somewhere.
I will fight through every waterfall of panic,
Chemicals engulfing me in their tsunami strength,
Every tipped-scale imbalance,
Past every overactive gland and through
The corridors of your logic, your learned behaviors,
The union of sight and seeing,
And I hope you see me,
I hope you trust what I have learned.
Your brain is too beautiful to stay terrified
Forever.

TEACHER NOTE Another compelling piece is Kobe Bryant's retirement letter "Dear Basketball," which was made into an animated film and won an Academy Award in 2018 for Best Animated Short Film. Both are available on the web and could be shown and read in conjunction with Katya's poem.

TRY THIS (as quickly and as specifically as you can for 2–3 minutes)

+ Write down all that comes to mind as you think of the extinction of all of these animals, or anything else that seems to be disappearing.

+ Begin writing from the line "One by one," "They shake our hands and step into the dark," "They move away and fade out of memory," or any other line, letting the line lead your thinking.

The Animals Are Leaving
by Charles Harper Webb

Ted Kooser, in *American Life in Poetry* (2009), says, "To read in the news that a platoon of soldiers has been killed is a terrible thing, but to learn the name of just one of them makes the news even more vivid and sad. To hold the name of someone or something on our lips is a powerful thing. It is the badge of individuality and separateness. Charles Harper Webb, a California poet, takes advantage of the power of naming in this poem about the steady extinction of animal species."

One by one, like guests at a late party
They shake our hands and step into the dark:
Arabian ostrich; Long-eared kit fox; Mysterious starling.

One by one, like sheep counted to close our eyes,
They leap the fence and disappear into the woods:
Atlas bear; Passenger pigeon; North Island laughing owl;
Great auk; Dodo; Eastern wapiti; Badlands bighorn sheep.

One by one, like grade school friends,
They move away and fade out of memory:
Portuguese ibex; Blue buck; Auroch; Oregon bison;
Spanish imperial eagle; Japanese wolf; Hawksbill
Sea turtle; Cape lion; Heath hen; Raiatea thrush.

One by one, like children at a fire drill, they march outside,
And keep marching, though teachers cry, "Come back!"
Waved albatross; White-bearded spider monkey;
Pygmy chimpanzee; Australian night parrot;
Turquoise parakeet; Indian cheetah; Korean tiger;
Eastern harbor seal; Ceylon elephant; Great Indian rhinoceros.

One by one, like actors in a play that ran for years
And wowed the world, they link their hands and bow
Before the curtain falls.

TEACHER NOTE   As a craft move, the more specific we are as a writer, the more vivid the writing is to a reader. Naming something lets the reader connect more strongly. Note also how the analogies to casual things we don't pay attention to emphasize our inattention to these losses.

Only Human
by Kerri B.

He sits over subway grates

Legs tucked up against his body

Wearing dirt-smudged khakis

And a ripped flannel shirt

That homeless man

Who reaches out his hand

And motions to a pan of pennies and nickels

That homeless man

Who people awkwardly step around

Not bothering to give a second glance

Like being poor is a disease

That can be caught

And spread

He sits

Like a stray dog

Flea-covered and matted

At night he curls in doorways

Aching with empty stomach pains

He is a veteran

A grandfather

A businessman

In need of love and care

He is a human being

Not a beggar

He speaks nothing but one plea

I beg of you

Feed me

TRY THIS (as quickly and as specifically as you can for 2–3 minutes)

+ Write out all that Kerri's words bring to mind for you.

+ Borrow any line, and write all that you can, letting the line lead your thinking.

+ Think about those things in the world that you try to ignore and "step around," because they make you uncomfortable. Write out what those things are, why they make you uncomfortable, and how you try to ignore them.

© 2018 by Linda Rief from *The Quickwrite Handbook: 100 Mentor Texts to Jumpstart Your Students' Thinking and Writing*. Portsmouth, NH: Heinemann.

TRY THIS (as quickly and as specifically as you can for 2–3 minutes)

+ Write anything that this piece brings to mind for you. What pops into your head as you hear the words of these two events?

+ Borrow any line or specifically the last two lines: ". . . are we even yet? Who's keeping score?" Let the line(s) lead your thinking as you write.

+ Use a date—year and month—to start the writing. A date that is significant to you. What is happening on that date? Write it in the present tense.

+ Think of an historical event in the distant or not-so-distant past—an event that had an indirect, direct, or no impact on you. Describe what you know and what you are curious about, even if what you write is all questions.

Who's Keeping Score?
by Linda Rief

It is 1988. The 4th of July. Washington, DC. I am on a writing fellowship from the Kennedy Center. On the Capitol steps I sit arm to arm, thigh to thigh, alone, among 350,000 strangers waiting for our national celebration. The man in front of me spreads the polished pages of an art book across his knees, tapping his left thumb across Gauguin's right ear to the beat of a Strauss waltz. To my right, a very pregnant young woman tries to find comfort on the concrete steps as she works out a crossword puzzle. With two hours to wait, I open *Unwinding the Vietnam War* and read John Ketwig's words: "I had seen body bags and coffins stacked like cordwood, had seen American boys hanging lifeless on barbed wire, spilling over the sides of dump trucks, dragging behind an APC like tin cans behind a wedding party bumper. I had seen a legless man's blood drip off a stretcher to the hospital floor and a napalmed child's haunting eyes. I knew the spirit of the bayonet and the sizzle of a rocket tearing across the night sky."

I close the book and lay it in my lap. I glance to my left. Two Japanese children lie on their stomachs, fat fingers gripping thick crayons. They fill in an American flag—cardinal red, royal blue, chalk white. Hot air hovers over the crowd. Several rows in front of me, a young man maneuvers into the crowd, settling down on the steps between two families. He pulls *The Washington Post* from his back pocket and lifts the front page to read. The headline says: *U.S. Navy blows plane out of sky*. The article is accompanied by a picture of two Iranian children crying, clutching each other at the Dubai Airport, as their parents' bodies are netted like flounders from the Persian Gulf.

The National Symphony Orchestra begins and 350,000 people stand to sing "God Bless America." Flashes of reds, whites, and blues boom and sizzle across the night sky. I too stand, because I love my flag, and I love my country. I wonder though, are we even yet? Who's keeping score?

It is 2001. The 11th of September. A beautiful day on the east coast of the United States. Warm. Cloudless sapphire sky. I am a teacher in a small town in New Hampshire. On the drive into school I roll down the window to breathe in the touched-by-autumn air.

During the day I hear, and see, the horrific news. A plane has slammed into the World Trade Center in New York City. I watch as a second plane slices through the second tower of concrete and steel and glass, like a knife through butter. Fire and smoke roll and billow into the sky as a small child in Manhattan runs from the window of his school five blocks away. "Teacher, teacher—the birds are on fire!"

That night the headlines read: *America Attacked! Planes Hijacked! World Trade Center is No More!*

Wednesday September 12th, 2001. Warm. Cloudless sapphire sky. In school I too stand, hand over heart, for the Pledge of Allegiance. I love my flag. I love my country. But I wonder, are we even yet? Who's keeping score?

© 2018 by Linda Rief from *The Quickwrite Handbook: 100 Mentor Texts to Jumpstart Your Students' Thinking and Writing.* Portsmouth, NH: Heinemann.

TRY THIS (as quickly and as specifically as you can for 2–3 minutes)

✦ Write out anything this excerpt brings to mind for you.

✦ Start with the line "I knew little about" and let the line lead your thinking.

✦ Thinking about pets or any animals you have been associated with or known, what intrigues you, makes you curious, impresses you about some things they can do?

Excerpt from *The Soul of an Octopus*
by Sy Montgomery

On a rare, warm day in mid-March, when the snow was melting into mud in New Hampshire, I traveled to Boston, where everyone was strolling along the harbor or sitting on benches licking ice cream cones. But I quit the blessed sunlight for the moist, dim sanctuary of the New England Aquarium. I had a date with a giant Pacific octopus.

I knew little about octopuses . . . But what I did know intrigued me. Here is an animal with venom like a snake, a beak like a parrot, and ink like an old-fashioned pen. It can weigh as much as a man and stretch as long as a car, yet it can pour its baggy, boneless body through an opening the size of an orange. It can change color and shape. It can taste with its skin. Most fascinating of all, I had read that octopuses are smart. This bore out what scant experience I had already had; like many who visit octopuses in public aquariums, I've often had the feeling that the octopus I was watching was watching me back, with an interest as keen as my own.

How could that be?

Moonlight Ghosts
by Jesse S.

The bulbous eyes emerged like fireflies, yellow and vivid, in the ghostly night. The light radiating from the lustrous moon filtered through the canopy of towering trees. A thin layer of fog blanketed the surface of the rocky terrain. Soft hoots from owls pierced the dead silence, as if a warning call that danger was lurking nearby.

An abrupt movement from the thick brush caught the yellow eyes of the gray creature. The massive wolf locked onto its prey. The small doe staggered in her attempt to escape. It was too late. Steel jaws clamped down tightly on the neck of the helpless deer. Ghostly howls echoed through the canyon walls like sad songs. Then, silence.

Savage cruelty? Survival?

TRY THIS (as quickly and as specifically as you can for 2–3 minutes)

✦ Write down all that comes to mind from Jesse's words.

✦ Write down your thinking with respect to Jesse's questions: "Savage cruelty? Survival?"

✦ Borrow any phrase or line and write out all that comes to mind, letting the line lead your thinking.

TRY THIS (as quickly and as specifically as you can for 2–3 minutes)

✦ Write down anything Ben's poem brings to mind for you.

✦ Borrow any line, letting the line lead your thinking.

✦ Think of a book you've read that changed your thinking about yourself or the world in which we live. Start your writing with the phrase "On reading" and describe how the book affected your thinking, your beliefs, or your feelings.

The White Flakes
(On Reading *Schindler's List*)
A Found Poem
by Ben W.

Low creeping fog spreads

Across the ground, like a vine

Sucking the life

Out of the air

A shiver blows

From barracks to barracks

These are no hotels

But holding tanks of fuel for

The furnace

Each living

Breathing

Human

Turned to puffs of smoke under

The night's sky

Children play

In the endless snowflakes

Catching them on their tongues

Only stopping

Because these little white flakes

Never melt

TEACHER NOTE A found poem is created from a text that the poet "finds" and recasts as a poem, deleting words while retaining the strongest nouns and verbs that create the most vivid imagery and feelings. The poet decides where to break lines, how to arrange lines, and how to space words and lines so that the text looks and reads like a poem, rather than prose.

This is a complete response to "The White Flakes." After reading this poem, Sariel wrote this in her writer's-reader's notebook. As we studied social justice issues, specifically the Holocaust, I thought surely she would expand on this, but she chose not to. Perhaps some day she will—or has.

My grandfather was sent to Auschwitz when he was barely older than me. One of his jobs was to go with the other boys and cart the corpses through the town to a pit on the other side (of the camp). Every day he noticed the windows were shut in the town, the shutters drawn.

Decades later, after the war was long over, my grandfather was on a research trip in South Africa. One day he sat with another German man and they began sharing war stories. After my grandfather told this man his story, the man, looking white, shaken, and sweaty, got up and walked away. He walked into the desert.

A few days later he found my grandfather. "I lived in that town," he said. "I was a young boy. Every morning my mother told me to close the shutters at the exact same time—every morning. I never understood why, but never asked. I wondered what went on out there."

It was not always neglect. Not always pretending to not notice "an elephant in the room." Sometimes it was just not understanding. Not realizing, or being hidden from the truth. I, a Jewish girl, granddaughter of a Holocaust survivor, realize this. Sympathy with everyone, understanding every point of view, is very important.

Excerpt from *Station Eleven*
by Emily St. John Mandel

TRY THIS (as quickly and as specifically as you can for 2–3 minutes)

- Write anything this excerpt brings to mind for you.

- Borrow any line or phrase, letting the line lead your thinking and writing.

- Starting with the phrase "No more _____," fill in the space and write out what you would miss most if *that* (whatever *that* is) caused all of this to happen.

AN INCOMPLETE LIST

No more diving into pools of chlorinated water lit green from below. No more ball games played out under floodlights. No more porch lights with moths fluttering on summer nights. No more trains running under the surface of cities on the dazzling power of the electric third rail. No more cities. . . .

No more screens shining in the half-light as people raise their phones above the crowd to take photographs of concert stages. No more concert stages lit by candy-colored halogens, no more electronica, punk, electric guitars.

No more pharmaceuticals. No more certainty of surviving a scratch on one's hand, a cut on a finger while chopping vegetables for dinner, a dog bite.

No more flight. No more towns glimpsed from the sky through airplane windows, points of glimmering light; no more looking down from thirty thousand feet and imagining the lives lit up by those lights at that moment. No more airplanes, no more requests to put your tray table in its upright and locked position—but no, this wasn't true, there were still airplanes here and there. They stood dormant on runways and in hangars. They collected snow on their wings.

No more countries, all borders unmanned.

No more fire departments, no more police.

No more Internet. No more social media, no more scrolling through litanies of dreams and nervous hopes and photographs of lunches, cries for help and expressions of contentment and relationship-status updates with heart icons whole or broken, plans to meet up later, please, complaints, desires, pictures of babies dressed as bears or peppers on Halloween. No more reading and commenting on the lives of others, and in so doing, feeling slightly less alone in the room.

TEACHER NOTE Read this excerpt and the excerpt (on the next page) from *The Hitchhiker's Guide to the Universe* together, asking your students to try one of the suggestions given on each page.

Excerpt from
The Hitchhiker's Guide to the Universe
by Douglas Adams

"And what happened to the Earth?"

"Ah. It's been demolished."

"Has it," said Arthur levelly.

"Yes. It just boiled away into space."

"Look," said Arthur, "I'm a bit upset about that."

Ford frowned to himself and seemed to roll the thought around in his mind. "Yes, I can understand that," he said at last.

TRY THIS (as quickly and as specifically as you can for 2–3 minutes)

+ Thinking about this conversation and the *Station Eleven* excerpt, write out the first thing that comes to mind when you think about the future of the world.

TRY THIS (as quickly and as specifically as you can for 2–3 minutes)

+ Write out anything Emma's writing brings to mind for you.

+ Borrow any line, one that resonates with you or causes you to think about your own life, your own experiences. Let the line lead your thinking.

+ Look at the following lines. "Guilt at living in such an excessive culture," "I see the way poverty crushes dreams," "the way my abundance of money creates them." What do these lines bring to mind for you?

Riendo, Llorando, y Viviendo en el Mundo
(Laughing, Crying, and Living in the World)
by Emma W.

A single tear slips down my cheek.
It hangs on the end of my chin, waiting to fall.
I press my head against the glass window,
Straining my neck for a last look
At the place I have come to love
With such an unexpected passion.

In the past two weeks,
I have aged far beyond my fourteen years.
Everything I believed, everything I thought, or tried not to think,
        collided.
My world turned upside down,
And I fell off the cliff of blissful ignorance,
And dropped into a chasm of wonder, intensity
And salsa at every meal.

I let go of the things that I worried about.
They all seemed so trivial now.
Will I finish my homework in time to get to my piano lesson to
        clean my room and buy the new outfit for band to practice
        to study to worry . . .
Who would want to learn the quadratic formula when there was
        a world to see?
What good is the Molecular Kinetic Theory when you don't have
        safe drinking water?

I realized I had been holding my breath for so long,
And I just needed to exhale.

I cried more in these two weeks than I ever had in my life.
Tears
Of guilt at living in such an excessive culture,
Of the realization that the world is big, so much broader than my mind
     could grasp.
I see the way poverty crushes dreams,
The way my abundance of money creates them.
Tears of already missing those I had just met.

And so many tears of a friendship that was so wonderful, I never wanted
To let go.

So here I sit, my forehead pressed against the glass of the airplane
     window,
Straining my neck for a last look at the place I have come to love
With such an unexpected passion.
I catch a last glimpse of Cochabamba, an image forever cemented
In my memory,
The perfect valley, surrounded by the majestic Andes.
The Taquina brewery perched on the hill,
Its whitewashed walls in contrast
To the green of the mountain framing it, the brown of the homes below it.
The Cristo stands watch over the city,
Welcoming me in so kindly
And I feel a sense of relief.
He is bidding me farewell,
But

I won't be gone long.

© 2018 by Linda Rief from *The Quickwrite Handbook: 100 Mentor Texts to Jumpstart Your Students' Thinking and Writing*. Portsmouth, NH: Heinemann.

TRY THIS (as quickly and as specifically as you can for 2–3 minutes)

+ Write out all that comes to mind as a result of this poem.

+ Borrow a line (for example, "I saw one once," "It lay like a great sadness," "It was hard to breathe," "I stopped knowing how to measure my own grief"), letting the line lead your thinking.

+ Write out all the questions that come to mind as a result of these whales beaching themselves. How would you answer those questions?

Echolocation
by Sally Bliumis-Dunn

The whales can't hear each other calling
in the noise-cluttered sea: they beach themselves.
I saw one once—heaved onto the sand with kelp
stuck to its blue-gray skin.
Heavy and immobile

it lay like a great sadness.
And it was hard to breathe with all the stink.
Its elliptical black eyes had stilled, were mostly dry,
and barnacles clustered on its back
like tiny brown volcanoes.

Imagining the other whales, their roving weight,
their blue-black webbing of the deep,
I stopped knowing how to measure my own grief.
And this one, large and dead on the sand
with its unimaginable five-hundred-pound heart.

Excerpts from *The Outsiders*
By S. E. Hinton

I could picture hundreds and hundreds of boys living on the wrong sides of cities, boys with black eyes who jumped at their own shadows. Hundreds of boys who maybe watched sunsets and looked at stars and ached for something better. I could see boys going down under street lights because they were mean and tough and hated the world, and it was too late to tell them that there was still good in it, and they wouldn't believe you if you did. It was too vast a problem to be just a personal thing. There should be some help, someone should tell them before it is too late. Someone should tell their side of the story, and maybe people would understand then and wouldn't be so quick to judge a boy by the amount of hair oil he wore.

. . . I sat down and picked up my pen . . . remembering . . . a handsome, dark boy with a reckless grin and a hot temper. A tough, towheaded boy with a cigarette in his mouth and a bitter grin on his hard face . . . a quiet, defeated-looking sixteen-year-old whose hair needed cutting badly and who had black eyes with a frightened expression to them. . . . I wondered for a long time how to start writing about something that was important to me. And I finally began like this: . . . .

TRY THIS (as specifically and as quickly as you can in 2–3 minutes)

+ Write down anything these excerpts bring to mind for you.

+ Borrow any line, letting the line lead your thinking as you write.

+ S. E. Hinton wrote *The Outsiders* more than fifty years ago, yet her description of boys she saw and knew and felt so strongly about still holds true today. Too many boys—and girls—are still judged for what they wear and how they look, and not for who they are inside. What do her words bring to mind for you and all you see around you in your world today?

+ Borrow Hinton's last two lines from this excerpt, writing about something that is important to you.

TRY THIS (as quickly and as specifically as you can for 2–3 minutes)

+ Take the phrase "evening light" and write out all that the line brings to mind.

+ Borrow any other line or word and let the line/word lead your thinking.

Evening Light
by Lynn S. Adams

Evening light takes me to the blush red hues of sunset

Running barefoot through the grass in my grandparents' backyard

Our feet blackened by our time in the sun and Missouri dirt

The grass becomes dewy in sharp contrast to the concrete driveway

    Still holding July heat

Fireflies, evading us, dart away from our every move

    As we try to capture their magic in a jar

Temporary magic—you have to let them go

Evening light becomes heat lightning

Deep dark reds and purple in the distance

Lightning with no resounding thunder

Evening light makes the small wooded area between Gram's

    And the neighborhood pool suddenly

Unfamiliar

Dark

Mysterious

Playing tag in the dry creek bed

The clay crumbles under tanned toes

The shadows offer hiding places where previously there were none

Evening light calls us in to take a bath

Evening light washes off chlorine, sunscreen, clay, grass, heat and sweat

Evening light tells us Tomorrow we can do it all again

TEACHER NOTE Share any of the writing in the Interlude that follows to show your students the variety of ways students wrote in response to "Evening Light." These pieces of writing could also be mentor texts from which your students could find writing.

© 2018 by Linda Rief from *The Quickwrite Handbook: 100 Mentor Texts to Jumpstart Your Students' Thinking and Writing.* Portsmouth, NH: Heinemann.

On the next few pages read Claire's poem, "Fireflies," and notice how she borrowed Lynn S. Adam's line "Temporary magic—you have to let them go," from which to write. Notice also how she uses the repetition of the fireflies with, "Light on. Light off," to carry us through the poem.

The poem "Night Walks" by Kaylie also began as a quickwrite with the phrase "evening light." Kaylie wrote fast, and through the process of redrafting again and again, came up with this poem, the phrase "evening light" no longer a part of the piece of writing.

Jane changed "Evening Light" to "Summer Night," reflecting on the longing she has to stay at Lake Erie with her grandparents, instead of returning to the realities of her life at home.

Dillon used "sunset" in place of "evening light" to describe this moment of awe at a boys' camp in Maine, a place where these boys are anything but reserved and quiet.

Read Claire's, Kaylie's, Jane's, and/or Dillon's pieces, either before or after doing a quickwrite in response to one or all, or to the phrase "Evening Light."

Fireflies
by Claire G.

Temporary magic—you have to let them go
Fireflies. Light on.

Light Off.

Evening light. Picture time. Memories. It all goes quick
From sunset to blackness. Don't you dare blink.

Evening light. Soar. Run. Fly. Catch their magic in a jar. And sleep with it by your side.
Brick by brick
Stone by stone
Grass stains, dirt marks
Feet pounding, never aching,
Nothing hurts while under
Evening light.

Smile after smile. Backyards. String lights. A glass of lemonade, and
a best friend by your side.
Still. Light on.

Light off.

A game.
Truth or Dare . . .
Circle. Grins. Light on.

Light off.

Evening light. Climb a tree. Sing a song.
Don't worry.
Nobody's listening.

Hide and Seek
Manhunt
Kick the Can.

Temporary magic—you have to let them go—
Fireflies. Light on.

Light off.

Night Walks
by Kaylie M.

When I was little
The sky danced with new stars
My dad bundled me up
And took me out for night walks

Cradled in his arms
He pointed out the Big Dipper
The Little Dipper
The North Star
Beetlejuice

I don't remember the story of Beetlejuice
But I remember it was significant
Because my dad pointed it out to me
Beetlejuice is yellow
Far away from Earth

And I know that the older you get

The more distant you become

Farther and farther away from those

Who captured you in their warm embrace

Never reluctant to offer comfort

When it was needed most

The stars

Glistened in the bright sky

Elegant

Full of life's greatest secrets

Cradled in his arms

Protected by his warm embrace

His breath cool against my cheek

We watched the stars spin

Above the earth and life as we knew it

Summer Night
by Jane R.

Evening light means walking down the tired, wooden stairs to the cement boardwalk with rusty sides, to the small pebbly beach, watching the sun fall off a pile of pink, orange, purple, and blue clouds into the lake's waiting depths. The small waves stroke the shore softly, and whoosh backwards in retreat.

Summer night means walking around the beach, picking up small brown sticks, smooth beach glass, and interesting stones. The small sticks are deposited into what will soon become a bonfire, and the glass and stones into an envelope on the walk for safekeeping. Once there is enough wood in the fire we ignite it, and what starts as a pathetic flicker grows to a hungry fire. We find thin sticks and pop fat white marshmallows on, turning them over the heat, and laughing when they catch fire. Sparks hurl themselves into the air, a never-ending game of who can go higher. The sky is navy blue now, and someone forgot to pick up the diamonds that have spilled, to glitter and float in the night sky, teasing the sparks.

My sister and I walk to the edge of the dock and watch for shooting stars. When we come back, the stories begin. I tell a tale of a young boy who finds Atlantis at the bottom of the lake by chance. My grandfather speaks of a young owl, my grandmother of a recent dream. We sit by the fire and soak in the serenity rolling off the lake like fog. All too soon the sticky s'mores are history, the sky is black, the fire is but embers, and Father Time can only make so many exceptions in life, so we pack up the chairs, and throw sand on the fire, and collect the envelope of beach glass.

As I begin to walk up those same weather-beaten wooden steps, I know that this time tomorrow everything will be a whirlwind, and I wish I could stay with my grandparents, the clear night air, the fireflies, and the glassy surface of a lake at night. But hockey and school and riding are calling my name, so I turn slowly and cast one last bittersweet, longing glance towards Lake Erie. Finally, I tear my gaze away and I swear I can feel my heart splitting too, but I dutifully climb the wooden stairs that lead back to reality.

© 2018 by Linda Rief from *The Quickwrite Handbook: 100 Mentor Texts to Jumpstart Your Students' Thinking and Writing*. Portsmouth, NH: Heinemann.

Sunset Over Little Huck
by Dillon M.

We shuffle through the twisted roots and rocks of the chapel in silence as the rain pounds on the towering pine trees above us. Our leader guides us to the dark outline of Conlin Lodge and as we ascend the stairs the darkness breaks into waves of deep reds and purples that reflect off the lake. As we turn the corner we see the full extent of the color palette that is the sunset. Deep blues and purples are on the periphery of my sight and as the colors blend towards the falling sun, they become a majestic maroon, and then a blood red that make a halo around the soft reds, oranges and yellows—the eye of the color display.

The glorious sky is a deep contrast to the dark blues and black of the vast lake and the independent greens of Farm Island. Little Huck radiates this vast color scheme and the luminous property of the beach makes the island look ablaze. Captivated by the splendor, we watch a lone boat glide over the plane of water, sending ripples through the glassiness of the lake. The waves ripple toward the moored sailboats, which bob in response. The waves continue their journey unheeded until they strike the mossy rocks beneath the porch.

We campers, young, male, and impulsive, sit reserved and motionless, characteristics unheard of, especially among the younger kids. We take in the majesty of the sunset and, perhaps some of us, contemplate the troubles of the universe.

Nobody wants to break the silence. Only when the sun finally dips below the horizon does anyone think to move.

TEACHER NOTE Before reading Gendler's excerpt, I ask students to list three qualities they have, or someone close to them has, that are positive qualities, such as *responsible*, *kind*. I ask them to then list three negative qualities they have, or someone they know has, that they wish they didn't have, such as *procrastinator, stubborn*.

TRY THIS (As quickly and as specifically as you can for 2–3 minutes)

+ Personify one of the traits you listed.

+ Think of a trait you really admire in someone else and wish you had. Write down that trait and personify what you think *he or she* looks like, acts like, believes.

Excerpt from *The Book of Qualities*
by J. Ruth Gendler

Compassion

Compassion wears Saturn's rings on the fingers on her left hand. She is intimate with the life force. She understands the meaning of sacrifice. She is not afraid to die. There is nothing you cannot tell her.

Compassion speaks with a slight accent. She was a vulnerable child, miserable in school, cold, shy, alert to the pain in the eyes of her sturdier classmates. The other kids teased her about being too sentimental, and for a long time she believed them. In ninth grade, she was befriended by Courage.

Courage lent Compassion bright sweaters, explained the slang, showed her how to play volleyball, taught her you can love people and not care what they think about you.

In many ways Compassion is still the stranger, neither wonderful, nor terrible, herself, utterly, always.

Fear

Fear has a large shadow, but he himself is quite small. He has a vivid imagination. He composes horror music in the middle of the night. He is not very social, and he keeps to himself at political meetings. His past is a mystery. He warned us not to talk to each other about him, adding that there is nowhere any of us could go where he wouldn't hear us. We were quiet. When we began to talk to each other, he changed. His manners started to seem pompous, and his snarling voice sounded rehearsed.

Two dragons guard Fear's mansion. One is ceramic and Chinese. The other is real. If you make it past the dragons and speak to him close up, it is amazing to see how fragile he is. He will try to tell you stories. Be aware. He is a master of disguises and illusions. Fear almost convinced me that he was a puppet maker and I was a marionette.

TEACHER NOTE For the quickwrite, you might use other qualities from Gendler's book and have students personify a quality associated with a topic you may be studying: social justice issues (perseverance, courage juxtaposed with fear, despair) as one example. Students can also take a quality they want to work on during the year and illustrate that quality so they see it and work on it continuously.

Energetic
by Grace H.

Energetic is a wild horse, trapped in the body of a tame beast. She rears when people are too loud; she screams when they are too quiet. Locked inside another body, she is only able to escape when they let her run. As she is led onto the track she prances with overflowing energy. Her jetblack mane changes colors as quickly as she changes moods: red when she's angry, blue when she's sad, and yellow when she's happy. Her heartbeat quickens. . . . She is pushed into the gate. She stamps and snorts waiting to be released.

The gate is opened. She is out like a lightning bolt, beautiful but too fast to see. She is a wild beast released. There is no getting her back. . . . She tears around the final bend with full speed. Her hooves thunder, ripping up the track, dirt flying, the world blurring around her. She blows past the finish line, thundering on, disappearing with the wind, as if she were never there.

Beautiful
by Grace H.

Beautiful is a feather in the wind or the sunset over the ocean. She drifts in the breeze and is as graceful as a flag dancing in the wind. Her colors reflect in the water like glass catching the light and she fills the sky with purple, pinks, and oranges. . . . She knows her flaws and accepts them. Beautiful is a role model for young girls, making them step back and realize that they too are beautiful in their own way. She encourages them to break out of their shells and be themselves. She is light, when everything is dark. She is colorful when everything is dull. She is happy when everyone is sad. She has an open heart and an open mind, ready to take on anything the world throws at her.

TEACHER NOTE Notice what several of my students and a teacher wrote to personify a personal trait. Use their examples if they are of help to your students. Grace and Annika's came down on paper as they appear here. Sometimes the best writing spills onto the page when we write fast. Michael (a teacher at the Kitigan Zibi School in Maniwaki, QC, Canada) went back to his several times, playing with line breaks, adding information, and deleting some lines to come up with his best draft.

Interlude

Jealousy
by Annika B.

Jealousy is a bitch, if you don't mind the word. Her face is a slab of ice with hard angles and a permanent scowl etched in, hiding behind stringy black hair. She lies and deceives, rots relationships, even the strongest kids. Between her victims she forces her witch's hands, insidiously, perfidiously. She pries them apart to fill her empty heart with the illusion of strength—*Jealousy must have strength*—to break a bond like that. But don't be fooled, Jealousy is nothing but weak.

Jealousy is a bitch,
> *If you don't mind the word.*
Her face, a slab of ice
With hard angles etched
Into a permanent scowl
Hiding behind stringy, black hair.
Jealousy lies and deceives,
Rots relationships—
> *Even the strongest kind.*
Between her victims.
She forces witch's hands,
Insidiously,
Perfidiously.
She pries them apart
To fill her own empty heart
With the illusion of strength.
> *She must have strength*
To break a bond like that.
But don't be fooled.
Jealousy is nothing
But weak

TEACHER NOTE In her writer's-reader's notebook, Annika wrote this quickwrite. Notice how she then turned it into a poem.

A Triumph of Faith
by Michael McPake

Anxiety.

He is the incessant whisper in your ear that you don't measure up.

He devotedly reminds you of your flaws, weaknesses, and liabilities.

He is neurotic and irrational, often inventing the ridicule of others.

He fancies himself a prophet of doom, envisioning innumerable futures plagued by loss, grief, and misery.

He has a fatal flaw, however.

It is his mortal enemy, Faith, whose presence he cannot endure. . . .

Faith, you see, offers a mother's calm and comforting embrace.

Faith, if you seek her, will always invite you into her house of refuge.

She offers you the wisdom of knowing that life shall unfold as it should.

She reminds you that, as an innocent child of the Universe, you deserve to be happy—and—you deserve to be loved.

She will rekindle within you the fire of your spirit, and wrap you in her warm blanket of serenity.

She will bless you with the vitality, resilience, and peace of mind that accompanies the focusing of your being in the here . . . in the now . . . in this miraculous moment of life.

© 2018 by Linda Rief from *The Quickwrite Handbook: 100 Mentor Texts to Jumpstart Your Students' Thinking and Writing*. Portsmouth, NH: Heinemann.

TRY THIS (as quickly and as specifically as you can for 2–3 minutes)

+ Write all that this poem brings to mind for you.

+ Borrow any line that resonates with you and let the line lead your thinking.

+ Abigail repeats the words *If only* a number of times. Take that line and write out all that comes to mind, letting that line lead your thinking.

If Only
by Abigail Lynne Becker

If only I could shelter you
From the pain,
The longing.
If only I could dry your eyes
And let you cry no more.

I'd wrap you tight
Inside my heart.
I'd listen on those darkening nights
When nothing sounds
But silence.
Creeping in through
The cracks in your soul—
Spilling out in a distorted jumble
Leaving you with nothing
But an overwhelming emptiness.

If only I could shelter you,
Keep you from the pain.
If only I could make the moment last.
I'd hold on tight
Inside my heart
Where pain would never
Find you.

Yet, the time has come
And gone again
And still, I am but a friend.

If I thought it would help,
I'd lie for you,
Take your pain, make it my own.
If I thought it would help,
I'd cry for you.

I'd take your strength, wind it tight
And spin it out into the world.

Everyone would know
You cannot be broken.

Kirsten J.

Looking Back

© 2018 by Linda Rief from *The Quickwrite Handbook: 100 Mentor Texts to Jumpstart Your Students' Thinking and Writing.* Portsmouth, NH: Heinemann.

First Memory
by Georgia Heard

TRY THIS (as quickly and as specifically as you can for 2–3 minutes)

+ Write out anything this vignette brings to mind for you.

+ Write down your first memory. Let this first memory simmer for a while. Go back to it and see if you can figure out what sits underneath that memory. Why is it memorable? Why do you think you remember it?

+ Georgia Heard asks: "Is there any significance to this image in your current life?" Write out what you think about any connections.

My sister and I are swinging on the swing sets in Texas. The sky is darkening, in the west it scowls a greenish black. The winds have started. My mother stands next to our small brick house on the base, her hair and skirt blowing, calling our names to come in. I hop off my swing and turn around to wait for my sister. She swings higher and higher, her legs sticking out straight in front of her. A tornado is coming. My mother can barely walk now because the wind is so strong. She walks toward my sister, who jumps off the swing, spraining her ankle. My mother carries her in her arms, and I follow behind.

This is the first conscious imprint on my mind. I was five and my father was in the army and stationed in Texas. A tornado was approaching and my sister wouldn't come inside. From the time I was born until that afternoon I had lived five years but I can't remember anything. What happened to these memories? This first memory is significant to me, the fact that I remember it at all. A storm coming. Perhaps I felt something in the air—my parents' eventual divorce, my tumultuous relationship with my sister when we were children.

Zits Cartoon

by Jerry Scott and Jim Borgman

TRY THIS (as specifically and as quickly as you can for 2–3 minutes)

✦ Write out anything that this *Zits* cartoon brings to mind for you.

✦ Start with the line "It seemed like a good idea at the time" or "you know how sometimes something that seems like a really good idea turns out to be not such a good idea" and let the line lead your thinking.

TEACHER NOTE If you look at page 156 in this book, you will see the piece titled "Tonsillectomy," which began as a quickwrite in my writer's-reader's notebook in response to this cartoon. With revision after revision it eventually became one of my best pieces. Share cartoons and pictures with your students. Ask them: What do you see? What do you notice? What do you think? What do you feel?

Snip
by Lucas S.

It seemed like a good idea at the time to give my cat a hair cut. I was an imaginative four-year-old then, and my cat had very long whiskers. I thought it was time to give him a trim.

My cat was in the bathroom drinking from his dish of water when the idea crossed my mind. His pink tongue lapped up the water as I snuck up behind him. A sleek black and white coat of fur covered his plump body. A pair of red scissors hid in my hands. I felt their smooth, cool plastic handle as I gripped them behind my back. Slowly, I crept closer and closer until I could easily reach out and touch him. I moved my hand that clutched the scissors closer. "Snip!" It was a clean cut.

A couple of long, translucent whiskers fell silently to the floor as my cat, Tobey, ran away in fear. It sounded like nails on a chalkboard as his claws skidded across the wood floor. One side of his face had long drooping whiskers while the other had barely any. I knew then that I was in deep trouble if anyone found out. I needed to find Tobey before anyone else did and trim the other whiskers off, too, so it wasn't as noticeable.

"Tobey . . . Tobey," I called out across the house. No response. He usually meows when we call his name. I ran quickly around the house checking everywhere for him. First, I peered under the beds. No luck. Next I ran to look under the couches. No Tobey. Finally, I bounded down the stairs and looked up to the ledge in front of the window. He loved to sit there and gaze at the birds, but not this time. Then I galloped up the stairs, and ran around the house looking everywhere again, becoming more and more frantic. My heartbeat quickened at the thought of someone finding him with a terrible haircut. The noise I was making from running around frantically, boomed through the house.

My mother was due to have a baby in a week, and she was very sick. She almost never took naps, but she must have dozed off by accident while she was

TEACHER NOTE "Snip" began in Lucas's writer's-reader's notebook, the place where he can play with ideas, as seen here. Once he knows this is the piece he wants to craft into a fully developed story, he takes it to the computer, to bring to a fuller piece that still goes through the process of revising and editing.

folding laundry. Startled awake by the ruckus, my mother came upstairs to check if I was all right. She walked up each step slowly and carefully. A line from lying on the pillow streaked across her cheek. She rubbed her drowsy eyes, asking "Lucas. Are you okay?" as she watched me run from place to place. "What are you looking for?"

"I'm looking for Tobey," I replied.

I paused for a second. The room fell silent. I knelt on the blue Oriental rug that lay across the hardwood floors in our living room. Little pieces of black and white Star Wars Legos were scattered across the carpet. I looked down at them while my heartbeat quickened; all my muscles tensed. A soft pitter-patter of pawsteps approached from behind us. Then, the dreaded sound stopped as a timid "meow" floated through the room. My eyes widened as my mom turned around to see the lopsided haircut staring up at her. I looked at Tobey again and saw the left side of his face with long, white whiskers; on the right side there was nothing but some tiny little stubs.

My mom's jaw dropped and she narrowed her eyes, as if trying to get a better view. Then her face changed and her mouth closed into an angry scowl. She furrowed her eyebrows. But, before she could speak, I ran to my room and locked the door behind me. I jumped into my bed and started screaming into my pillow. I felt a lump growing in my throat and I curled up into a ball on top of my Spider-Man bedspread. My favorite stuffed hippopotamus stared blankly at me, as if he was judging me for what I had done. I tossed him across the room. My mind whirled. I always hate doing something wrong, and it had begun to dawn on me that what I had done was very wrong.

The shadows of my Lego sets grew longer and longer as the sun fell towards the horizon. Finally, my father came home. I could hear some quiet murmurs from the other side of the door, and a loud, "What?!" Then came heavy footsteps

continues

Interlude

continued from previous page

down the hall. He unlocked the door with the key that always sat above the doorframe. The sound of metal on metal as the key clicked into place made my stomach tighten.

I was worried that he would start to yell, but instead, he spoke in a worried voice. "Luke, you know that cats need whiskers to sense their surroundings." I did not know that, but I nodded. I stared at his long tie to avoid looking at his frustrated brown eyes. "That was a very poor choice. I am disappointed." A long family talk then followed about the proper use of scissors. A hunt began for all the scissors in the house, even the little safety ones. They were corralled like little accomplices and put in their jail atop the fridge.

I thought it would have looked better if I had been able to cut the other side off. Tobey looked lopsided to me. But I decided not to say a word. It didn't take long for the whiskers to grow back, but it was four months before my parents allowed me to use scissors at home again.

Caden S.

© 2018 by Linda Rief from *The Quickwrite Handbook: 100 Mentor Texts to Jumpstart Your Students' Thinking and Writing*. Portsmouth, NH: Heinemann.

Bullfrogs
by David Allan Evans

For Ernie, Larry, and Bob

sipping a Schlitz
we cut off the legs,
packed them in ice, then
shucked the rest back into
the pond for turtles

ready to go home
we looked down and saw
what we had thrown back in:
quiet-bulging eyes nudging along
the moss's edge, looking up at us,

asking for their legs

TRY THIS (as quickly and as specifically as you can for 2–3 minutes)

+ Write down anything this poem brings to mind for you.

+ Borrow any line, letting the line lead your thinking.

+ Has there ever been a time when you felt guilty about something? Write out the scene, describing the incident as fully as you can.

© 2018 by Linda Rief from *The Quickwrite Handbook: 100 Mentor Texts to Jumpstart Your Students' Thinking and Writing.* Portsmouth, NH: Heinemann.

Interlude

Nita K., a teacher in Colorado, wrote the following vignette in response to "Bullfrogs," saying both she and her brother, now adults, still remember the incident vividly, still unable to shake the guilt. Every time I read it, my throat tightens.

Snowy Owl

Not of malice, but born of the curiosity of children, we chucked a hundred rocks, one after another at the nest. Grunting. Throwing. Gathering missiles that fell short or long of the mark. Throwing again and again and again. Never a protest from the nest. In the ensuing quiet, my brother shinnied the tree. Nose to beak, he looked into the wounded eyes of a snowy owl, courageously shielding the lifeless bodies of her downy babies.

Excerpt from *The Prince of Tides*
by Pat Conroy

When I was ten I killed a bald eagle for pleasure, for the singularity of the act, despite the divine, exhilarating beauty of its solitary flight over schools of whiting. It was the only thing I had ever killed that I had never seen before. After my father beat me for breaking the law and killing the last eagle in Colleton County, he made me build a fire, dress the bird, and eat its flesh as tears rolled down my face. Then he turned me in to Sheriff Benson, who locked me in a cell for over an hour. My father took the feathers and made a crude Indian headdress for me to wear to school. He believed in the expiation of sin. I wore the headdress for weeks, until it began to disintegrate feather by feather. Those feathers trailed me in the hallways of the school as though I were a molting, discredited angel.

"Never kill anything that's rare," my father had said.

"I'm lucky I didn't kill an elephant," I replied.

"You'd have had a mighty square meal if you had," he answered.

TEACHER NOTE You might read "Bullfrogs" by David Allan Evans first, have students quickwrite, read the anecdote by Nita, or the excerpt from Conroy, and ask your students to quickwrite again in response or reaction to either anecdote.

What Is Beauty?
by Madi M.

Becoming Me

Can she pull through? Will the fear be gone?
Or will the girl disappear, and the shell live on?

Beauty is not being so thin that people can see your spine. Beauty does not come from not eating. Calorie counting, the inability to be present with your family, and loneliness are not beautiful things. Constantly weighing yourself on the bathroom scale and doing workouts in your room do not give you a glow. There is no award for losing yourself. Empty smiles, being short-tempered and anxious, these things do not grant superiority.

And were you hoping for confidence? Did you expect a sense of pride and accomplishment from your struggles? Did you believe that control would come out of this? No, there is nothing involving happiness or greatness when the topic is eating disorders. Binging and purging, restricting, over-exercising, they do nothing to fill the hole. The temporary feeling of control is just that, just temporary.

But there is a way. There must be a way to be real again. And it is not by continuing the cycle and further increasing the harm you inflict on yourself and others. Relief only comes when you finally say *enough*, when you learn the true meaning of beauty.

TRY THIS (as specifically and as quickly as you can for 2–3 minutes)

+ Write out anything Madi's words bring to mind for you.

+ Borrow any line, letting the line lead your thinking.

+ Write out any of the ways you stay true to yourself.

+ Describe some of the obstacles you have overcome to stay true to yourself, and how you did that.

TRY THIS (as quickly and as specifically as you can for 2–3 minutes)

✦ Write out anything this vignette brings to mind for you.

✦ Borrow any line, letting the line lead your thinking.

On This Day Mom Is Happy
by Linda Rief

I am ten, and sitting in the back seat between my eight-year-old and four-year-old sisters. It is Sunday afternoon and we are driving to Nantasket for lunch/supper at Howard Johnson's. All four windows are wide open and the brisk breeze washes over me as we drive Route 3A to the beach.

I know there are white boats with blue tarps bobbing on their moorings in the harbor. I know the oak and maple trees along the route brush the sky with their broad leaves. I know the hum of tires on the hot pavement is the only sound I want to hear. I don't say anything. I don't want to separate us with words.

I sit forward and rest my left elbow on the back of dad's driver's seat and my right elbow on the back of mom's passenger seat. We are in the Buick, all five of us, a family going for an outing on a Sunday afternoon.

We are driving to Howard Johnson's where we won't go in, but dad will go to the Take-Out Window and order a pint of fried clams, a quart of French fries, and a large coke. He will ask politely for extra, extra, extra tartar sauce, three small cups, and a handful of napkins. None of us will whine or complain or ask for more clams or our own cokes or even our own plates when mom divides the clams and French fries onto napkins because all three of us know you can make French fries taste like fried clams if you dip them in tartar sauce, but really because we are together and each of us is smiling.

On this day mom is happy. On this day dad is sober.

TEACHER NOTE Ask students what they know about this family from the information given (and not given), especially before we get to the last two sentences. Turning the writing 180 degrees—to a place we didn't expect to go—tells us a lot of background information without actually saying it. This may take students longer than two or three minutes, but it might be worth asking them to try: Try to think of one scene that you can describe as fully as possible. To make it more immediate, write it in the present tense. With your last line or two, turn the writing 180 degrees, to a place the reader doesn't expect to go.

Good Bones
by Maggie Smith

Life is short, though I keep this from my children.
Life is short, and I've shortened mine
in a thousand delicious, ill-advised ways,
a thousand deliciously ill-advised ways
I'll keep from my children. The world is at least
fifty percent terrible, and that's a conservative
estimate, though I keep this from my children.
For every bird there is a stone thrown at a bird.
For every loved child, a child broken, bagged,
sunk in a lake. Life is short and the world
is at least half terrible, and for every kind
stranger, there is one who would break you,
though I keep this from my children. I am trying
to sell them the world. Any decent realtor,
walking you through a real shithole, chirps on
about good bones: This place could be beautiful,
right? You could make this place beautiful.

TRY THIS (as quickly and as specifically as you can for 2–3 minutes)

+ Write out anything this poem brings to mind for you.

+ Borrow any phrase (for example, "Life is short") or full line (for example, "For every bird there is a stone thrown at a bird" or "You could make this place beautiful") and write all that Smith's words bring to mind, letting the line lead your thinking.

TEACHER NOTE In the Interludes that follow, notice that my response to this poem is far less serious than Alyssa's. Mentor texts naturally elicit so many different responses.

Interlude

On Beauty
Alyssa Eckhardt

This place could be beautiful, right?
How many times did my mom wonder, how many times did she say to herself
I know I can make this beautiful?

Is there beauty in abuse, Mom?

Is there beauty in a man who, most nights, can't make it
from the couch to the bed?
Is there beauty in dumping out bottles before he comes home?
Where is the beauty in his rage once he finds out?

This place could be beautiful, right?

Where is the beauty in, *we will talk about this in the morning . . . when you are
    coherent?*
Where is the beauty in, *girls go to your room . . . now . . . please?*
Where is the beauty in those tears that slowly trickled down your cheeks.
Your hiccups were the only thing that gave you away.
Where is the beauty in seeing him treat a woman so differently,
now that you are gone?

© 2018 by Linda Rief from *The Quickwrite Handbook: 100 Mentor Texts to Jumpstart Your Students' Thinking and Writing*. Portsmouth, NH: Heinemann.

TEACHER NOTE Alyssa Eckhardt, a seventh- and eighth-grade language arts and reading teacher at Issaquah Middle School in the state of Washington, wrote her own response to "Good Bones" at a workshop I did in San Diego. Often when we write fast, we go directly to those topics that matter the most to us.

How many times did you say, *this could be beautiful*?

But Mom—I found it beautiful.
Guilt
How often does guilt come with beauty?

There was beauty because you were mine,
Alcohol doesn't like to share . . .
Great, I don't like to either.

There was beauty in our late night read-ins.
There was beauty in popcorn in bed.
There was beauty in homemade spa days.

There was beauty in knowing I came first.
I was always there.

We could call this place beautiful? Right?

Interlude

The first time I read "Good Bones," I borrowed the line "Life is short," and in my writer's-reader's notebook wrote a kind of labyrinth (a style I learned from Tom Romano). I am not sure what I will do with this, but it is there if I ever need it.

Life is short, and mine is getting shorter, so before I get on a plane I put the handwritten letter I received from E. B. White when I was ten inside my copy of *Stuart Little*, which I put on top of the handmade book I bought from an artist on Martha's Vineyard, an accordion book that is about haying and is filled with poetry, which I place in my favorite basket, the Nantucket basket I bought in Edgartown even though I gulped when the shop owner told me the price, so expensive I am afraid to write it, but maybe someone will figure it out from the ivory hinges on the maple handle and the small ivory disk scrimshawed with shells in the basket base and I put HUNTER's name in capital letters on a post-it note and carefully place it in the basket with the letter and the book so everyone knows if the plane goes down this belongs to my oldest grandson because I hope someday he will love books and baskets and words as much as I do but just in case I email my daughter-in-law and tell her that under no circumstances should she put any baskets she finds in my house in a yard sale for a quarter because even the tiny one no bigger than the tip of my thumb cost me more than four pounds of coffee beans from Breaking New Grounds.

How to Paint a Donkey
by *Naomi Shihab Nye*

She said the head was too large,

the hooves too small.

I could clean my paintbrush

but I couldn't get rid of that voice.

While they watched,

I crumpled him,

let his blue body

stain my hand.

I cried when he hit the can.

She smiled. I could try again.

Maybe this is what I unfold in the dark,

deciding, for the rest of my life,

that donkey was just the right size.

TRY THIS (as specifically and as quickly as you can for 2–3 minutes)

✦ Write out anything this poem brings to mind for you.

✦ Borrow a line, letting the line lead your thinking.

✦ Think of a time that someone's criticism stopped you from doing what you were doing—building something, drawing, writing, or making something. Describe what happened. What was said? What did you do?

Ria V.

Siakiva S.

TEACHER NOTE Notice the illustrations my students did in response to Nye's poem. Your students might enjoy illustrating their own writing in response to Nye's writing.

© 2018 by Linda Rief from *The Quickwrite Handbook: 100 Mentor Texts to Jumpstart Your Students' Thinking and Writing*. Portsmouth, NH: Heinemann.

Tonsillectomy

by Linda Rief

I set up my operating room on the back porch, carefully laying my utensils across the railing: towel, band aids, clothespin, needle and thread and scissors. I had dragged the chrome stool from the kitchen, grabbed a towel and band aids from the bathroom, and found a needle, thread and scissors in my mom's sewing box. The babysitter paid no attention to me each time I ran past her, as she was deeply engrossed in a book.

My four-year-old sister stood on the porch, eyes wide, watching me run in and out of the screen door as I set up my plan. I was two years older, six at the time, and she stuck to me like Velcro, doing anything I wanted her to do.

"I know how you can get ice cream every day for the next two weeks," I said to her. "Do you want to do it?"

"Uh-huh," was her only reply.

"Climb on the stool," I said. She gripped each step with her chubby fingers, turned around on the top step, and sat down. "Okay," I said, not sure where to begin. I tucked her straight hair behind her ears and pushed her bangs further up on her forehead. "Okay," I said again. I reached for the towel and carefully draped it around her neck. I fastened it with the clothespin. "Okay," I said again.

Several weeks earlier my mother had taken us across the street to visit Barbara Adams, our ten-year-old neighbor who had just had her tonsils out. We had a package of coloring books, crayons, and paper doll books to give her. I noticed that Barbara had a large bowl of vanilla ice cream in her lap. "It's all she can eat for the next few weeks," her mother said, when she noticed me gawking at the bowl. "It soothes her throat, which is really scratchy and sore."

My eyes widened. I had an idea.

TRY THIS (as quickly and as specifically as you can for 2–3 minutes)

✦ Write out anything this story brings to mind for you.

✦ Borrow any line, and write out all that the line brings to mind. Let the line lead your thinking, in any direction.

✦ Think of a time when you had what you thought was a good idea, but you were stopped or were *not* stopped in the nick of time from hurting yourself or hurting someone else. Write out all you can about that memory.

TEACHER NOTE This writing began as a quickwrite in response to the *Zits* cartoon on page 143. My students' reactions to the quickwrite and my telling the story made me want to write it down. I wrote, rewrote, reorganized, rewrote—always trying to keep the tension that gripped my students each time I told the story.

My sister sat wide-eyed on the stool. "Okay," I said. "Open wide." She did—her jaw dropped and I could see two rows of baby teeth. Without moving her head, her eyes traveled to the scissors as I picked the pair up from the railing and held them tight. Her eyes looked straight at me and then dropped down to the scissors in my hand. I hesitated. I wasn't sure where her tonsils were, but thought they might be that thing shaped like a lima bean hanging down at the back of her throat. "Okay," I said again, as I inserted the scissors into her open mouth.

I knew there might be blood, which is why I had the band aids. I didn't know exactly why I needed the needle and thread, but I did know my cousin needed stitches when he fell on the ice and cut his knee wide open. I wasn't really sure what would need stitching when I cut her tonsils out, or how I would go about it, but I was prepared just in case.

Just as I was about to snip, the screen door slammed shut behind me and I heard the babysitter's voice. "Don't you move an inch!" My sister's head jerked. The scissors snapped shut. Blood bubbled up from her lower lip, where the scissors had snipped as they closed in my hand.

I have no recollection of what the babysitter did, what my parents did to me, or what my little sister was thinking. She—my sister—did, however, get even with me for most of the rest of our lives together.

TRY THIS (as specifically and as quickly as you can for 2–3 minutes)

+ Write out anything this poem brings to mind for you.

+ Borrow any line, letting the line lead your thinking.

+ What does Collins make you think about when he says, "This is the beginning of sadness."

+ When you were four or seven or nine or any age, what did you pretend or imagine or believe or do, that has somehow lost its importance or its delight now that you are older?

On Turning Ten
by Billy Collins

The whole idea of it makes me feel
like I'm coming down with something,
something worse than any stomach ache
or the headaches I get from reading in bad light—
a kind of measles of the spirit,
a mumps of the psyche,
a disfiguring chicken pox of the soul.

You tell me it is too early to be looking back,
but that is because you have forgotten
the perfect simplicity of being one
and the beautiful complexity introduced by two.
But I can lie on my bed and remember every digit.
At four I was an Arabian wizard.
I could make myself invisible
by drinking a glass of milk a certain way.
At seven I was a soldier, at nine a prince.

But now I am mostly at the window
watching the late afternoon light.
Back then it never fell so solemnly
against the side of my tree house,
and my bicycle never leaned against the garage
as it does today,
all the dark blue speed drained out of it.

This is the beginning of sadness, I say to myself,
as I walk through the universe in my sneakers.
It is time to say good-bye to my imaginary friends,
time to turn the first big number.

It seems only yesterday I used to believe
there was nothing under my skin but light.
If you cut me I would shine.
But now when I fall upon the sidewalks of life,
I skin my knees. I bleed.

© 2018 by Linda Rief from *The Quickwrite Handbook: 100 Mentor Texts to Jumpstart Your Students' Thinking and Writing*. Portsmouth, NH: Heinemann.

TRY THIS (as specifically and as quickly as you can for 2–3 minutes)

+ Write out anything this excerpt brings to mind for you.

+ In what ways is this philosophy an admirable stance to take for any of us in the way we live our lives?

+ In what ways might someone disagree with this philosophical stance?

+ Borrow any line or phrase or sentence, letting the line or phrase or sentence lead your thinking.

Excerpt from *Lone Survivor*
by Marcus Luttrell

Their lives stand as a testimony to the central paragraph of the philosophy to the U.S. Navy Seals: I will never quit. I persevere and thrive on adversity. My Nation expects me to be physically harder and mentally stronger than my enemies. If knocked down, I will get back up, every time. I will draw on every remaining ounce of strength to protect my teammates and to accomplish our mission. I am never out of the fight.

Making a Mark
by Emily Geltz

I used to bite my sister,

sink my teeth

into her pudgy, baby arm.

In timeout,

my chair an island

in the ocean of the kitchen floor,

I tell my mom it's because she's soft.

She swears it's because I'm jealous.

Either way,

at least

I made a mark.

Now, as I navigate

the shores of my existence,

any steps I take are

washed away

by an incoming tide.

I yearn to make a lasting impression,

take hold of something and sink my teeth into it.

TRY THIS (as quickly and as specifically as you can for 2–3 minutes)

+ Write out anything this poem brings to mind for you.

+ Borrow a line—"I used to bite my sister," "in timeout," "I yearn to make a lasting impression"—or any other line, letting the line lead your thinking.

+ Write down Emily's last two lines of the poem. If those were your lines, what would they mean to you?

© 2018 by Linda Rief from *The Quickwrite Handbook: 100 Mentor Texts to Jumpstart Your Students' Thinking and Writing.* Portsmouth, NH: Heinemann.

TRY THIS (as quickly and as specifically as you can for 2–3 minutes)

+ Think of a time when you did something you probably shouldn't have done, and might have even regretted before you did it. Stick with one scene from that story, as if you are setting the scene for the bigger movie. Show the reader what you see, hear, smell, touch, taste, and think.

+ Borrow the line "What have (or had) I done?" or any line, and write from that, letting the line lead your thinking.

From the First Hello to the Last Goodbye
by Linda Rief

It's 11:45 PM and the central speaker that rumbles through Paragon Park has begun to play "From the First Hello to the Last Goodbye"—the signal to close shop. I grab the rag that smells of Monday on this Saturday night and begin to wipe down the fountain. Frappe cans. Chocolate syrup. Spilled vanilla ice cream. The scrape of metal legs against the concrete floor surprises me. I look up. Eddie Andrews smiles at me. He has flipped the wrought iron chair around and sits straddled over the seat. Waiting. He's waiting. Waiting for me.

He wears tight jeans, black motorcycle boots, well worn at the left heel. His hair is slicked back in a D-A. A pack of Marlboros is wound tightly into the T-shirt sleeve of his left arm, right above the tattoo I do not want to read.

The merry-go-round has slowed to a stop. The empty benches at the top of the Ferris Wheel rock back and forth. Even Kate Smith is silenced to static. What have I done?

Eddie holds the stubby end of a cigarette between his index finger and thumb, lifting it to his lips where he inhales so deeply I think he has swallowed this cancer stick. He lifts his chin, purses his lips, and lets the exhaled smoke drift skyward. He flicks the still smoldering butt onto the sidewalk. He smiles at me. I smile back at him.

Eddie is waiting for me. I have lied to my parents. I don't remember what I said so they wouldn't wait up. I don't remember how I told Fran and Brad I wouldn't need a ride home tonight. I don't remember why I agreed to go out with this bad boy from Hull. I don't even remember when or how I met him.

The amusement park slows into midnight on the smells of cotton candy, vanilla frappes, and steamed hotdogs.

I toss the rag in the sink, step from behind the fountain, and let Eddie wrap his arm around my shoulder. He leans in too close to my face. Stale cigarettes and too many beers smell like rotting fish. Teeth and tongue—his and mine—crash together. I try not to gag.

What have I done? How can I anger my father if he doesn't know who I am with?

TEACHER NOTE When Stephen King's son was seven, he fell in love with Bruce Springsteen's E Street Band, particularly with Clarence Clemons, the band's sax player. King and his wife bought Owen a tenor sax for Christmas and lessons with a local musician.

Excerpt from *On Writing*
by Stephen King

Seven months later I suggested to my wife that it was time to discontinue the sax lessons, if Owen concurred. Owen did, and with palpable relief—he hadn't wanted to say it himself, especially not after asking for the sax in the first place, but seven months had been long enough for him to realize that, while he might love Clarence Clemons's big sound, the saxophone was simply not for him. . . .

I knew, not because Owen stopped practicing, but because he was practicing only during the periods Mr. Bowie had set for him. . . . Owen mastered the scales and the notes—nothing wrong with his memory, his lungs, or his eye-hand coordination—but we never heard him taking off, surprising himself with something new, blissing himself out. And as soon as his practice time was over, it was back into the case with the horn. . . . What this suggested to me was that when it came to the sax and my son, there was never going to be any real play-time; it was all going to be rehearsal. That's no good. If there's no joy in it, it's just no good. It's best to go on to some other area, where the deposits of talent may be richer and the fun quotient higher.

Talent renders the whole idea of rehearsal meaningless; when you find something at which you are talented, you do it (whatever *it* is) until your fingers bleed or your eyes are ready to fall out of your head. Even when no one is listening (or reading or watching), every outing is a bravura performance, because you as the creator are happy. . . . (That goes) for playing a musical instrument, hitting a baseball, or running the four-forty.

TRY THIS (as quickly and as specifically as you can for 2–3 minutes)

+ Write out anything this anecdote brings to mind for you.

+ What is something you thought you wanted to do but realized at some point you were only going to "rehearsal" and were never really "blissing" yourself out? Write out what you were doing, and when and how you knew it just wasn't for you.

+ What is an activity—throwing a baseball, running, playing an instrument, reading, practicing with a lacrosse stick, drawing, coding—that you spend every spare minute doing? What do you do and how does that activity give you such pleasure?

© 2018 by Linda Rief from *The Quickwrite Handbook: 100 Mentor Texts to Jumpstart Your Students' Thinking and Writing*. Portsmouth, NH: Heinemann.

TEACHER NOTE On the blog *Teachers Write* (June 25, 2013), Kate Messner (an author of young adult books) suggests imagining a place that you love. It can be your kitchen or backyard, a faraway beach, a bustling city market, or a hard-to-reach vista at the end of a hike. She suggested that you start by writing this: *Sometimes (in your place, wherever you are), . . .* Then brainstorm all the things you might see, hear, smell, feel, taste, and wonder in that place. Notice that Catherine Flynn took the same word *Sometimes* and wrote about snow, something that she usually loves; yet, she admits that she isn't too sad when spring finally arrives.

TRY THIS (as quickly and as specifically as you can for 2–3 minutes)

+ Take the single word *sometimes* and write all that comes to mind.

Sometimes
by Kate Messner

Sometimes, on a mountain in April
The rocks are so slippery
You have to slow down
And this is good.
It's when you'll notice
A quiet curtain of moss
That drips with melting snow.
It's when you'll hear the rush
Of streams,
Swooping up tired old leaves
Carrying them off
In dizzy laughter
To somewhere warmer,
Open, free.

TEACHER NOTE You might pass around a stack of photographs or pictures that have an emotional feel to them and ask the students to step into the picture and write about it by starting with the word *sometimes*. Or ask students to bring in a photograph of a person or place to which they have a strong emotional attachment and write about this picture by starting with the same word *sometimes*. As Kate Messner says, the idea here is to mine

Sometimes Snow . . .

by Catherine Flynn

Sometimes snow
whispers itself into the world,
falling gently to the ground,
muffling every sound.
> Sometimes snow
> ROARS through the air,
> the north wind sculpting it
> into undulating drifts.

Sometimes snow
settles on tree branches,
offering itself to
thirsty blue jays.
> Sometimes snow
> is blue in the moon's glow,
> catching stark shadows,
> crisp as X-rays.

But then, come March,
snow begins to
melt.
At first just a trickle,
then a torrent,
filling brooks and
streams and rivers,
washing away
our winter weariness,
welcoming spring.

some memories and focus on sensory language. To the thinking of these two talented writers, I add (in inviting the students to write) the "Try This" suggestions:

+ If you love science, try "Sometimes in an electron field . . ." or any phrase that is related to science.

+ If you love history, try "Sometimes on the cobblestone streets of Boston . . ." or any phrase that is related to history or current events.

+ If you love math, try "Sometimes a binomial factor . . ." or any other phrase that is related to math.

© 2018 by Linda Rief from *The Quickwrite Handbook: 100 Mentor Texts to Jumpstart Your Students' Thinking and Writing.* Portsmouth, NH: Heinemann.

Sometimes just one word can spark an entire piece that needs little to make it better. It did for Emmy. Share her piece with your students to show them this is why we have to use all kinds of ways to find writing that matters to them. Sometimes one word can do it.

Sometimes
by Emmy G.

Sometimes you don't know where you're going. Sometimes you get lost on a mountain or lost in the woods or lost in your own thoughts. Sometimes your dad thinks he knows where he's going and turns east instead of west. Sometimes the road looks so long that there may not even be a destination. Sometimes you don't know how to pronounce onomatopoeia or spell "surprise." Sometimes you walk into a room and forget why you walked into that room because it's the kitchen and you're not even hungry. Sometimes you get caught up in your musings. Sometimes you just don't know.

Sometimes things are strange. Strange how you can see someone everyday and how they become so familiar to you and one day they just aren't there. Strange how it's not even a gap or a hole where they should be, just something the passage of time washed away. Strange how traditions can become "remember whens." Strange how we're always nostalgic for something. Strange how we're always looking forward to something.

Strange how summer can symbolize an end, and a goodbye, but we're always waiting for it. Strange, like the pattern we always fall into with the same people and places and things day after day, and then suddenly we aren't even home anymore and home is just the place where we grew up. Strange like the heaviness of memories and how they hurt our chests, even the happy ones. Strange how nothing stays the same forever.

© 2018 by Linda Rief from *The Quickwrite Handbook: 100 Mentor Texts to Jumpstart Your Students' Thinking and Writing.* Portsmouth, NH: Heinemann.

Sometimes things happen. People fight and tests are failed and shoes are forgotten at home. Dictators die and empires fail. Sometimes we learn a lot about writing but still can't put our words in the right order. Shirts shrink in the dryer. Books tear and water runs mascara. We say the wrong things and we hurt the wrong people and stuff falls apart. We run out of band-aids. Lamps break. Sometimes we lose and sometimes we don't deserve our wins. There are ups and downs. Sometimes we get scared.

But sometimes we find things. We find acceptance for who we are, despite all of our flaws. We look deep within ourselves and find forgiveness for people who have made us nothing but bitter. We find light and possibility in a place that was previously dark. We find peace, letting go of things that we've been holding onto for far too long. We find familiar things, people and places that were once strange. We find old things and turn them into new things again. We find pencils in our backpacks and dollars in our pockets. We find ourselves in the words we learn to put together. We find appreciation for beautiful places.

So yeah, sometimes you don't know where you're going. But that's okay. Because no matter how hard or crazy it seems, you're going to end up somewhere.

© 2018 by Linda Rief from *The Quickwrite Handbook: 100 Mentor Texts to Jumpstart Your Students' Thinking and Writing.* Portsmouth, NH: Heinemann.

How Angel Peterson Got His Name
by Gary Paulsen

TRY THIS (as quickly and as specifically as you can for 2–3 minutes)

✦ Write out anything this vignette brings to mind for you or anyone you know.

✦ What comes to mind if you start with the line "It's something we have to do" or "It was something I had to do"?

I had written a book about my life with my cousin Harris and talked about Harris peeing on an electric fence. The shock made him do a backflip and he swore he could see a rainbow in the pee. Many readers, especially women, were amazed that a boy would be insane enough to do this and didn't believe that it had happened. However, I did get many letters from men saying that either they or a brother or cousin or friend had tried the same stunt, with some exciting results. One man said it allowed him to see into the past.

I was sitting writing one day when my son, then thirteen, came into the house with a sheepish look on his deathly pale face. As he passed me, I couldn't help noticing that he was waddling.

"Are you all right?" I asked.

He nodded. "Sure. . . ."

"Why are you walking so funny?"

"Oh, no reason. I was doing something out by the goat barn and thought I'd try a little experiment. . . ."

"Pee on the electric fence?"

He studied me for a moment, then nodded. "How did you know?"

"It's apparently genetic," I said, turning back to work. "It's something some of us have to do. Like climbing Everest."

"Will I ever stop doing things like this?"

And I wanted to lie to him, tell him that as he grew older he would become wise and sensible, but then I thought of my own life: riding Harley motorcycles and crazy horses, running Iditarods, sailing single-handed on the Pacific.

I shook my head. "It's the way we are."

"Well," he sighed, tugging at his pants to ease the swelling, "at least I know what *that's* like and don't have to pee on any more fences."

And he waddled into his room.

TEACHER NOTE Before doing this quickwrite, you might read the passage from the book *Harris and Me* (page 126–132) that Gary Paulsen is referring to (it takes more than ten minutes to read) and have your students do a quickwrite in response. (What does that passage bring to mind for you? Or someone you know?)

The Idea Is Better Than the Truth
by Martha R.

I like the idea of spring,

Light showers, green buds, and the thawing earth.

But the truth is so different,

Brown slush, rotting leaves, and mud . . . mud . . . mud.

I like the idea of summer,

Pink lemonade, the smell of cut grass, and dripping popsicles.

But the reality is,

Sunburns, mosquitoes, and crowded public beaches.

I like the idea of fall,

Airborne kites, vibrant leaf piles, and geese flying south.

But it's not at all the same,

Raking wet leaves, whipping winds, and wood to stack.

I like the idea of winter,

Hat and mittens, iced trees, and a roaring fire.

But it's not at all like that,

Dangerous black ice, power lines down, and snow days

To make up in June.

TRY THIS (as quickly and as specifically as you can for 2–3 minutes)

+ Use Martha's structure of "I like the idea of . . . But the truth is. . . ." for describing something that can be seen from two very different perspectives.

+ Write out anything this poem brings to mind for you.

+ Write out the way you view the different seasons, whether it is from likes or dislikes.

+ Use her title "The Idea Is Better Than the Truth," letting that line lead your thinking.

© 2018 by Linda Rief from *The Quickwrite Handbook: 100 Mentor Texts to Jumpstart Your Students' Thinking and Writing*. Portsmouth, NH: Heinemann.

TRY THIS (as specifically and as quickly as you can for 2–3 minutes)

+ Write out anything Abby's poem brings to mind for you.

+ Borrow any line, letting the line guide your thinking as you write.

+ Start with the line "I always knew I loved _____, but I didn't know I loved _____," writing out the strongest remembrances of those things.

In the World of Forgetfulness
By Abby T.

I always knew I loved to read
The way the words give way to images in my mind
Each novel like a new adventure to be had
The enticing rustle and snap of a freshly opened book
Propped up on my pillow at dusk

But I didn't know I loved candles
The saturating fumes of soft gray smoke
Rising from illuminating towers of wax
Perhaps I only love the way they smell
The variety of evergreen sweetness
that colors my nostrils
Perfuming the house and home
Perhaps I love the flame
The way it dances and twirls each time I breathe
Guarding the house against the darkness

I know I love my mother's homemade bread
Even as I am swallowing it
Savoring the wholesome, homey taste
I love the way the yeast smells as the loaf rises
Pale like a newborn's bottom
The way the knife coats it
In a fine layer of pale, moist yellow butter

Sometimes I love my cats, though not
When I have to clean the litter box
And always the furry shape of Chubs
As he nestles into the curve of my spine while I read a good book
As warm as a hot water bottle

TEACHER NOTE Abby's piece began as a quickwrite in response to Linda Pastan's poem "Things I Didn't Know I Loved: After Nazim Hikmet," which can be found in her poetry collection *Queen of a Rainy Country* (2006).

And I love Shadow, the feisty way he bats
Furiously at a string dragged along the wood floor
Not willing to give up
And how can I not love my dog Trooper
His fierce, protective bark
And the way he runs up and jumps on us
when we get home from school
Always begging for a kiss

But how about the sight of old pictures
Those ancient black-and-whites
Like warring dark and light
Reminding me of things lost and never done
Missing, crying, and wailing for remembrance
In the world of forgetfulness

This is the haunting way time shows us
What really matters
Day and night
It is the kind of sadness and bitter happiness
I can touch
Stroking the smooth, pale cheeks of ice
Gazing
Down at the gentle, smiling faces
Of the loved ones I never knew
Peering out at me through a photograph
Eyes glittering with a hidden joy
That I never knew I loved

© 2018 by Linda Rief from *The Quickwrite Handbook: 100 Mentor Texts to Jumpstart Your Students' Thinking and Writing*. Portsmouth, NH: Heinemann.

TRY THIS (as quickly and as specifically as you can for 2–3 minutes)

+ Pick any line to start your own "How to Live," by getting close to the strongest images, specific tastes, and experiences.

+ Describe what you have done or want to make sure you do in your lifetime.

+ Simply start with the phrase "How to live" and write out your directives as to what is most important for anyone to do—from your perspective.

+ Describe the places you've been. Show us the contrasts from place to place.

+ Tom Romano in *Write What Matters* (2015, 95) invites his students to turn the writing into their own version: "How to dance," "How to play football," "How to fake read," "How to write," or how to do any other activity. Using Romano's suggestion, turn "How to Live" into something more specific and describe what you need to do.

Excerpt from "How to Live"
by Charles Harper Webb

"I don't know how to live."
        —Sharon Olds
Eat lots of steak and salmon and Thai curry and mu shu
pork and fresh green beans and baked potatoes
and fresh strawberries with vanilla ice cream.
Kick-box three days a week. Stay strong and lean.
Go fly-fishing every chance you get, with friends

who'll teach you secrets of the stream. Play guitar
in a rock band. Read Dostoyevsky, Whitman, Kafka,
Shakespeare, Twain. Collect Uncle Scrooge comics.
See Peckinpah's Straw Dogs, and everything Monty Python made.
Love freely. Treat ex-partners as kindly

as you can. Wish them as well as you're able.
Snorkel with moray eels and yellow tangs. Watch
spinner dolphins earn their name as your panga slam-
bams over glittering seas. Try not to lie; it sours
the soul. But being a patsy sours it too. . . .

Don't be too sane. Work hard. Loaf easily. Have good
friends, and be good to them. Be immoderate
in moderation. Spend little time anesthetized. Dive
the Great Barrier Reef. Don't touch the coral. Watch
for sea snakes. Smile for the camera. Don't say "Cheese."

Interlude

How to Live
(in the style of Charles Harper Webb)
by Brittany McNary Thurman

Drive a manual car—one without power
steering. Eat steak, but eat granola
too. Forget about your dark past. Drink
lattes made with half and half. Don't panic
when your car won't start. Live

Next door to friends. Or your sister. Or
become friends with your neighbors.
When you read a good book, eat chocolate.
(Good books demand chocolate.) Send
one letter a week, and always seal

it with a wax monogram. Kiss your niece.
Paint your nails brown if you want to.
Learn how to make your dad's pancakes
and your mom's pies. And road trip.
Don't ever forget to road trip. Touch

the Grand Canyon with your smile. Sit
outside in a cornfield in the bed of a truck,
and sit out there long enough to see
falling stars. Take a bottle of Muscato.
On the first snowfall each year,

embrace the heat of a fireplace
and the company of your favorite author.
Whatever you do in this life, stay away
from screens. Live a three-dimensional
life. Hold your beloved's face in your hands.

TEACHER NOTE After discussing Webb's poem and noticing how he wrote five-line stanzas, in which the last line of each stanza bled into the first line of the next stanza, one of Tom Romano's (2015, 95–96) college seniors, Brittany McNary Thurman wrote her own "How to Live" using the same style. You might point this out to your students, asking them to try that craft move in their own writing.

© 2018 by Linda Rief from *The Quickwrite Handbook: 100 Mentor Texts to Jumpstart Your Students' Thinking and Writing*. Portsmouth, NH: Heinemann.

Interlude

Taste, Touch, Travel
by Ella G.

Eat lots of gnocchi, gelato, Scotch eggs, and stuffed artichokes. Drink strong coffee and syrupy chocolate milk, frothed with a spoon. Listen to the Sox game on a battered old transistor radio, go to craft fairs and try on all the jewelry, learn how to roller skate and master the art of dancing with a heavy saucepan. Make early-morning eggs and bacon, drag up a chair to stand on so you can flip the crackling food with a spatula. Have family over every other day to laugh and trade stories and eat all you can of Nanny's homemade lasagna with rich marinara sauce. Sing loudly along to an off-key version of "Sweet Caroline" and spend rainy days playing board games by candlelight.

Spend a year in South Boston.

Fork up warm burritos and rice and soft cooked potatoes for breakfast, all covered in spicy sauces. Sip thick, cinnamony horchata and sweet, crisp hibiscus nectar. Pour yourself a nice big glassful with ice, and take it with you to the beach, it's only a few yards away. Sit in the warm water of the Pacific Ocean, draw messages in the sand, collect seashells and dodge coconuts as they plunk down on your walk home. Pore over novels on the balcony hammock, rocking in the glow of yet another brilliant sunset. Spot lizards on the walls and keep all the windows wide open, welcoming in the tropical air.

Spend a week in Mexico.

TEACHER NOTE Notice what Ella did in "Taste, Touch, Travel," building on her quickwrite to develop a more polished creative essay. The writing grew more and more complete as she added new places where she lived. Ideas sat in her writer's-reader's notebook until she needed them. The piece grew from questions and suggestions from her peers and from me, which built on the initial quickwrite of several lines about one place. Notice also how she ties all these places back together with one more memory of each place.

Eat homemade biscuits, crumbly oat cakes, strawberry jam, and fresh, buttery lobster. Drink cold, frothy milk and steep sweet tea to share with lots of family, add plenty of honey and cream. Pick the bedroom with the secret vent opening up to the kitchen and press your ear against it after bedtime to hear the stamping and singing and bright fiddle music. Make friends with a retired race horse named Firecat, jig on a fishing boat rocking on the ocean, your feet thumping to the heartbeat of the waves. Drive back country roads looking for abandoned schoolhouses, tiptoe over smooth stones by the sea, looking for sea glass, taste the tang of saltwater on your tongue.

Spend a week in Nova Scotia.

Fly in airplanes often, keep a journal about the adventures you've had, take as many photographs as your camera can hold, and hang them up on your wall when you get home. Experiment with glue and tissue paper and colorful beads. Mess around with glitter and shiny rhinestones on thick paper. Make scrapbooks and picture albums to share with family and friends when they come to visit. Try to recreate the food that you had, the scents you experienced, the music you heard. Make souvenirs into decorations, keep others in jewelry boxes and in plastic bins under your bed. Let your last vacation be your new happy place, return to it in your dreams, close your eyes and remember:

The crashing ocean waves in Mexico,

The sweet-smelling grassy fields in Nova Scotia,

The pockmarked, gritty sidewalks of South Boston,

And by then, you'll know how to live.

Afterword

Emerson advised us never to read a whole book, for there are too many and life is short. We should, he said, sip the best pages we find, and then close the book and move on. He advocated a kind of intellectual hunting and gathering. A deer does not consume the whole prairie, but takes the most tender and nutritious buds the earth offers, knowing by experience which flavors best give life.

So writing is really an act of reading. You read the landscape of your life and find the places where grief, or fear, or sudden surprise has revealed your truth. Then by reading the best of this experience, you write down one way to tell it. Then you read your first draft to find the places where the language is most your own, most in keeping with what your life revealed. There you have it. Revision is fully active reading, a way to carve your true voice from the words your hands have written.

—Kim Stafford (2003, 78–79)

I write to find what I have to say. I edit to figure out how to say it right.

—Cheryl Strayed (author of *Wild*)

What do students do with these quickwrites? They do what they would do with any piece of writing—reread to find the "nutritious buds . . . that best give life" to all they want to say, need to say. They choose the pieces to extend, to nurture, to take to a best draft. They revise and edit to figure out "how to say it right."

For many students, just finding *what* to say is the hard part. For many others, *how* to say what they need to say is the hard part. For many students, and for me, every bit of writing is the hard part.

Why do it? Because there is fulfillment and understanding and pleasure in clarifying our thinking to ourselves and in communicating our thoughts, our beliefs, our feelings to others. We are living in a world where our ability to understand each other is vital. Writing and reading give us the means to do just that. They give us voice. The better students are as readers and writers, the stronger they are as imaginative, creative, articulate, and compassionate citizens of the world.

Chart for Identifying Craft Moves in the Mentor Pieces

Title of Writing	Craft Move(s)	How Does This Impact the Writing and/or the Reader?
Example: "One Breath"	• Short sentences juxtaposed with long sentences • Using countdown—three minutes, etc.	• Like inhaling/exhaling— Shows his nervousness • Increases anxiety— Builds tension that reader can feel

Go back to the piece of writing that surprised you the most or that you liked the most, and try one or more of the craft moves you noticed to make the writing stronger and better.

© 2018 by Linda Rief from *The Quickwrite Handbook: 100 Mentor Texts to Jumpstart Your Students' Thinking and Writing*. Portsmouth, NH: Heinemann.

Chart for Identifying Craft Moves in the Mentor Pieces

Title of Writing	Craft Move(s)	How Does This Impact the Writing and/or the Reader?

Go back to the piece of writing that surprised you the most or that you liked the most, and try one or more of the craft moves you noticed to make the writing stronger and better.

Resources

ᔈ

Works Cited

Adams, Douglas. 1979. *The Hitchhiker's Guide to the Universe*. New York: Del Ray Press.

Ahmed, Samira. 2018. *Love, Hate & Other Filters*. New York: Soho Teen.

Alexander, Kwame. 2014. *The Crossover*. New York: Houghton Mifflin Harcourt.

Anderson, Laurie Halse. 2002. *Catalyst*. New York: Penguin Group.

Barnett, Mac, and Jory John. 2015. *The Terrible Two*. New York: Amulet Books.

Becker, Abigail Lynne. "Edge of Life" and "If Only." *A Box of Rain*. South Berwick, ME. Self-Published.

Bliumis-Dunn, Sally. 2018. "Echolocation." *Echolocation*. Asheville, NC: MadHat Press.

Bragg, Rick. 2002. "OLYMPICS: Skeleton Plunges Face-First Back Into the Winter Games." *New York Times*, Feb.18. www.nytimes.com/2002/02/18/sports /olympics-skeleton-skeleton-plunges-face-first-back-into-the-winter-games.html.

Brown, Daniel James. 2013. *The Boys in the Boat*. New York: Penguin Group.

Bryant, Kobe. 2015. "Dear Basketball." *The Players' Tribune*. November 29. https://www.theplayerstribune.com/en-us/articles/dear-basketball.

Capote, Truman. 1966. *A Christmas Memory*. New York: Random House.

Carey, Kevin. 2016. "Getting It Right." *Jesus Was a Homeboy*. New Jersey: Cavan Kerry Press.

Cisneros, Sandra. 1989. *The House on Mango Street*. New York: Random House.

Colasanti, Susane. 2009. *Waiting for You*. New York: Penguin Group.

Collins, Billy. 1995. "On Turning Ten." *The Art of Drowning*. Pittsburgh, PA: University of Pittsburgh Press.

Conroy, Pat. 1986. *The Prince of Tides*. Boston, MA: Houghton Mifflin Co.

Dailey, Jo'lene. 2018. "Column 612: What I Want to Do Most of the Time by Jo'lene Dailey." From *American Life in Poetry*, edited by Ted Kooser. Accessed January 23, 2018. www.americanlifeinpoetry.org/columns/detail/612.

De Fina, Allan A. 1997. "When a City Leans Against the Sky." *When a City Leans Against the Sky*. Honesdale, PA: Boyds Mills Press.

Dillard, Annie. 1989. *The Writing Life*. New York: Harper & Row.

Donnelly, Jennifer. 2003. *A Northern Light*. Orlando, FL: Harcourt.

Ellison, James. 2000. *Finding Forrester*. New York: Newmarket Press.

Evans, David Allan. 1991. "Bullfrogs." In *Poetspeak: In their work, about their work,* edited by Paul Janeczko. New York: Simon and Schuster.

Fassler, Joe. 2016. "To Write, Stop Thinking." *The Atlantic*. April 19. www.theatlantic.com/entertainment/archive/2016/04/kathryn-harrison-joseph-brodsky-by-heart/478791/.

Fletcher, Ralph. 2016. "The Last Time I Bumped Into Don Murray." *The Writer's Desk* (blog). January 25. http://livethewritinglife.blogspot.com/2016/01/the-last-time-i-bump-into-don-murray-by.html.

Flynn, Catherine. 2015. "SOL & Poetry Friday: Sometimes Snow…" *Reading to the Core* (blog). March 6. https://readingtothecore.wordpress.com/2015/03/06/sol-poetry-friday-sometimes-snow.

———. 2015. "Reply to the Question." *Reading to the Core* (blog). September 18. https://readingtothecore.wordpress.com

Galloway, Steven. 2008. *The Cellist of Sarajevo*. New York: Riverhead Books.

Gantos, Jack. 2005. "The Follower." In *Guys Write for Guys Read: Boys' Favorite Authors Write About Being Boys*, edited by Jon Scieszka. New York: Viking.

Gendler, J. Ruth. 1984. *The Book of Qualities*. New York: Harper & Row.

Glenn, Mel. 1982. "Rosemarie Stewart" and "Norman Moskowitz." *Class Dismissed!* New York: Clarion Books.

———. 1986. "Paul Hewitt." *Class Dismissed II*. New York: Clarion Books.

Hall, Meredith. 2007. *Without a Map*. Boston, MA: Beacon Press.

Heard, Georgia. 1995. "First Memory." *Writing Toward Home*. Portsmouth, NH: Heinemann.

Hinton, S. E. 1995 (1967). *The Outsiders*. New York: Penguin Group.

Hopkins, Ellen. 2011. *Perfect*. New York: Margaret K. McElderry Books.

Johnson, Angela. 2003. *the first part last*. New York: Simon and Schuster.

Kay, Sarah. 2014. "Hands" (YouTube video). May 10. www.youtube.com/watch?v=kqCMHcdYR_E.

Kearney, Meg. 2005. "Two Mothers." *The Secret of Me*. New York. Persea Books.

King, Stephen. 2000. *On Writing*. New York: Scribner.

Kooser, Ted. 2009. "American Life in Poetry: Column 203" *American Life in Poetry*. The Poetry Foundation. www.americanlifeinpoetry.org/columns/detail/203.

LaMott, Anne. 1994. *Bird by Bird*. New York: Pantheon Books.

Lange, Erin Jade. 2012. *Butter*. New York: Bloomsbury Children's Books.

Lobanov-Rostovsky, Sergei. 2016. "Editor's Notes and Cover Art: The Poetics of Science." *Kenyon Review online*. www.kenyonreview.org/journal/septoct-2016/index/.

Lowry, Lois. 1993. *The Giver*. New York: Houghton Mifflin.

Luttrell, Marcus. 2007. *Lone Survivor*. New York: Little, Brown and Company.

Lyon, George Ella. 1999. *Where I'm From*. Spring, TX: Absey & Co.

Mack, Marlo. 2015. "How to Be a Girl." www.howtobeagirlpodcast.com/videos.

Mandel, Emily St. John. 2014. *Station Eleven*. New York: Vintage Books.

McNair, Wesley. 1983. "Where I Live." *The Faces of Americans in 1853*. Columbia, MO: University of Missouri Press.

Merriam, Eve. 1976. "Reply to the Question: 'How Can You Become a Poet?'" *Rainbow Writing*. New York: Atheneum.

Messner, Kate. 2013. "Tuesday Quickwrite: Sometimes. . ." *Teachers Write* (blog), June 25. www.katemessner.com/teachers-write-625-tuesday-quick-write -sometimes.

Mills, Joseph. 2010. "The Husband." *Love and Other Collisions*. Winston-Salem, NC: Press 53.

Montgomery, Sy. 2015. *The Soul of an Octopus*. New York: ATRIA Paperback.

Murchison, Ginger. 2016. "Roller Coaster." *a scrap of linen, a bone*. Winston-Salem, NC: Press 53.

Murray, Donald M. 1996. *Crafting a Life in Essay, Story, Poem*. Portsmouth, NH: Boynton-Cook Publishers.

Nelms, Sheryl L. 1981. "City Life." *Iowa Woman* (November). Iowa Woman Endeavors, Inc.

Nelson, Jandy. 2010. *The Sky is Everywhere*. New York: Penquin Random House.

Newkirk, Tom, and Penny Kittle. 2013. *Children Want to Write: Donald Graves and the Revolution in Children's Writing*. Portsmouth, NH: Heinemann.

Okita, Dwight. 1995. "In Response to Executive Order 9066." *Crossing with the Light*. Sylmar, CA: Tia Chucha Press.

Pasricha, Neil. 2010. *The Book of Awesome*. New York: G.P. Putnam's Sons.

Pastan, Linda. 2006. "Things I Didn't Know I Loved: After Nazim Hikmet." *Queen of a Rainy Country*. New York: W. W. Norton.

Paulsen, Gary. 1993. *Harris and Me*. Orlando, FL: Harcourt Brace & Co.

———. 2005. "How Angel Peterson Got His Name." In *Guys Write for Guys Read: Boys' Favorite Authors Write About Being Boys*, edited by Jon Scieszka. New York: Viking.

Reynolds, Jason, and Brendan Kiely. 2015. *All American Boys*. New York: Atheneum Press.

Rief, Linda. 2003. *100 Quickwrites: Fast and Effective Freewriting Exercises That Build Students' Confidence, Develop Their Fluency, and Bring Out the Writer in Every Student*. New York: Scholastic.

———. 2007. *Inside the Writer's-Reader's Notebook*. Portsmouth, NH: Heinemann.

Riggs, Ransom. 2011. *Miss Peregrine's Home for Peculiar Children*. Philadelphia, PA: Quirk Books.

Romano, Tom. 2015. "My Father's Voice." *Write What Matters*. Oxford, Ohio: Tom Romano.

Rosenthal, Amy Krouse. 2005. *Encyclopedia of an Ordinary Life*. New York: Three Rivers Press (Random House).

Ruiz, Rene. 2000. "He Shaved His Head." In *You Hear Me?*, edited by Betsy Franco. Cambridge, MA: Candlewick Press.

Rylant, Cynthia. 1982. *When I Was Young in the Mountains*. New York: Puffin Books (Penguin).

Sáenz, Benjamin Alire. 2012. *Aristotle and Dante Discover the Secrets of the Universe*. New York: Simon and Schuster.

Scott, Jerry, and Jim Borgman. 2012. *Zits* (comic). February 26. Distributed by King Features. http://zitscomics.com/comics/february-26-2012/.

Skolnick, Adam. 2016. *One Breath*. New York: Crown Archetype.

Sloan, Holly Goldberg. 2013. *Counting by 7's*. New York: Puffin Books.

Smith, Ethan. 2014. "A Letter to the Girl I Used to Be" (YouTube video). www.youtube.com/watch?v=Lkn06Y8prDU.

Smith, Maggie. 2017. "Good Bones." *Good Bones*. North Adams, MA: Tupelo Press.

Stafford, Kim. 2003. *The Muses Among Us*. Athens, GA: The University of Georgia Press.

Stafford, William. 1966. "Traveling Through the Dark." *Ask Me: 100 Essential Poems*. New York: Harper & Row.

———. 1998. *The Way It Is*. Saint Paul, MN: Graywolf Press.

Stein, Garth. 2008. *The Art of Racing in the Rain*. New York: Harper.

Strayed, Cheryl. 2012. *Wild: From Lost to Found on the Pacific Coast Trail*. New York: Vintage Books (Random House).

Updike, John. 2009. "Baseball." *Endpoint and Other Poems*. New York: Alfred A. Knopf.

Van Draanen, Wendelin. 2011. *The Running Dream*. New York: Random House.

Webb, Charles Harper. 1991. "Swinging the River." In *Preposterous*, edited by Paul Janeczko. New York: Orchard Books.

———. 2006. "The Animals Are Leaving" and "How to Live." *Amplified Dog*. Pasadena, CA: Red Hen Press.

Wyrick, Jean. 2006. "Poem for an Inked Daughter." *UU World Magazine* XX (3). https://www.uuworld.org/articles/poem-an-inked-daughter.

Yoon, Nicola. 2015. *Everything, Everything*. New York: Random House.

———. 2016. *The Sun is Also a Star*. New York: Delecorte Press.

Zinsser, William. 1980. *On Writing Well*. New York: Harper & Row.

Additional Resources in Which I Find Material for Quickwrites

Appelt, Kathi. 2002. "The Tattoo Dragon." *Poems from Homeroom*. New York: Henry Holt.

Atwell, Nancie. 2006. *Naming the World*. Portsmouth, NH: Heinemann.

Buchwald, Emilie, and Ruth Roston, eds. 1987. *This Sporting Life: Contemporary American Poems About Sport and Games*. Minneapolis, MN: Milkweed Editions.

Fletcher, Ralph. 1997. *Ordinary Things: Poems from a Walk in Early Spring*. New York: Atheneum Books.

Janeczko, Paul. 1983. *Poetspeak: In their work, about their work*. New York: Bradbury Press.

Knudson, R. R., and May Swenson, eds. 1988. *American Sports Poems*. New York: Orchard Books.

Lyon, George Ella. 2013. *Many-Storied House*. Lexington, KY: The University Press of Kentucky.

Nye, Naomi Shihab, ed. 1992. *This Same Sky: A Collection of Poems from around the World*. New York: Four Winds Press.

Nye, Naomi Shihab, ed. 1999. *What Have You Lost?* New York: Greenwillow Books.

Paschen, Elise, and Dominique Raccah, eds. 2010. *Poetry Speaks: Who I Am*. Naperville, IL: Sourcebooks.

Rosenthal, Amy Krouse. 2016. *Textbook Amy Krouse Rosenthal*. New York: Dutton.

Rylant, Cynthia. 1994. *Something Permanent*. New York: Harcourt Brace & Co. (Photographs by Walker Evans)

Any poems, excerpts from novels, children's picture books, short essays, and vignettes that are language-rich, strong in sensory imagery, evoke strong feelings, are thought-provoking, and relevant to students' own experiences are valuable as resources for quickwrites.

Additional Resources

Rief, Linda. 2014. *Read Write Teach: Choice and Challenge in the Reading-Writing Workshop.* Portsmouth, NH: Heinemann.

This book describes my entire curriculum and has a description about quickwrites.

Rief, Linda. 2007. *Inside the Writer's-Reader's Notebook.* Portsmouth, NH: Heinemann.

Students need a place to collect and build on their writing/reading ideas. This is the *Writer's-Reader's Notebook* my students use in which to collect their quickwrites. This book, which contains many examples of my students' quickwrites, comes with a copy of the notebook itself. (It is a two-book set, although the notebooks themselves can be purchased through Heinemann in five-notebook packs.)

Credits

continued from page iv